CAMPAIGN 289

BURMA ROAD 1943–44

Stilwell's assault on Myitkyina

JON DIAMOND ILLUSTRATED BY PETER DENNIS
Series editor Marcus Cowper

First published in Great Britain in 2016 by Osprey Publishing,
PO Box 883, Oxford, OX1 9PL, UK
PO Box 3985, New York, NY 10185-3985, USA
E-mail: info@ospreypublishing.com

A CIP catalog record for this book is available from the British Library.

ISBN: 978 1 4728 1125 7
PDF e-book ISBN: 978 1 4728 1126 4
e-Pub ISBN: 978 1 4728 1127 1

Editorial by Ilios Publishing Ltd, Oxford, UK (www.iliospublishing.com)
Index by Alan Rutter
Typeset in Myriad Pro and Sabon
Maps by Bounford.com
3D bird's-eye views by The Black Spot
Battlescene illustrations by Peter Dennis
Originated by PDQ Media, Bungay, UK
Printed in China through Worldprint Ltd.

16 17 18 19 20 10 9 8 7 6 5 4 3 2 1

ARTIST'S NOTE

Readers may care to note that the original paintings from which the color
plates in this book were prepared are available for private sale. The
Publishers retain all reproduction copyright whatsoever. All enquiries
should be addressed to:
Peter Dennis, Fieldhead, The Park, Mansfield, Notts, NG18 2AT, UK
The Publishers regret that they can enter into no correspondence upon this
matter.

A NOTE ON JAPANESE AND CHINESE NAMES

In line with Japanese and Chinese customary practice, surnames precede
forenames/given names for those nationals mentioned in this work (e.g.
Lieutenant-General Tanaka Shinichi, referred to as Tanaka, and Lieutenant-
General Sun Li-jen, referred to as Sun).

THE WOODLAND TRUST

Osprey Publishing are supporting the Woodland Trust, the UK's leading
woodland conservation charity, by funding the dedication of trees.

AUTHOR'S ACKNOWLEDGMENTS

The author wishes to recognize the excellent editorial assistance and
collegiality of Nikolai Bogdanovic. His stellar contributions to the
composition of this book are ubiquitous. Also, the author realizes that
without the artistic vision of Peter Dennis, conceptual ideas about the
appearance of Burmese ground and air combat would have remained
solely as thoughts.

LIST OF ACRONYMS AND ABBREVIATIONS

ATC	Air Transport Command
CAI	Chinese Army in India (*Chih Hui Pu*)
CBI	China-Burma-India
C-in-C	commander in chief
COI	Coordinator of Information
CCS	Combined Chiefs of Staff
FEAF	Far East Air Forces
GOC	General officer commanding
HMG	heavy machine gun
I&R	Intelligence and Reconnaissance
IE	Indian Engineers
IJA	Imperial Japanese Army
IJAAF	Imperial Japanese Army Air Force
LMG	light machine gun
LRP	long-range penetration
MC	Military Cross
MTF	Myitkyina Task Force
NCAC	Northern Combat Area Command
OSS	Office of Strategic Services
RA	Royal Artillery
RASC	Royal Army Service Corps
RE	Royal Engineers
SEAC	South East Asia Command
SMLE	Short Magazine Lee-Enfield
USAAF	United States Army Air Force
USAMHI	United States Army Military History Institute

Key to military symbols

Army Group; Army; Corps; Division; Brigade; Regiment; Battalion; Company/Battery; Platoon; Section; Squad; Infantry; Artillery; Cavalry; Airborne; Unit HQ; Air defence; Air Force; Air mobile; Air transportable; Amphibious; Anti-tank; Armour; Air aviation; Bridging; Engineer; Headquarters; Maintenance; Medical; Missile; Mountain; Navy; Nuclear, biological, chemical; Ordnance; Parachute; Reconnaissance; Signal; Supply; Transport movement; Rocket artillery; Air defence artillery

CONTENTS

The eastern Indian states, Burma and Yunnan Province in southwest China

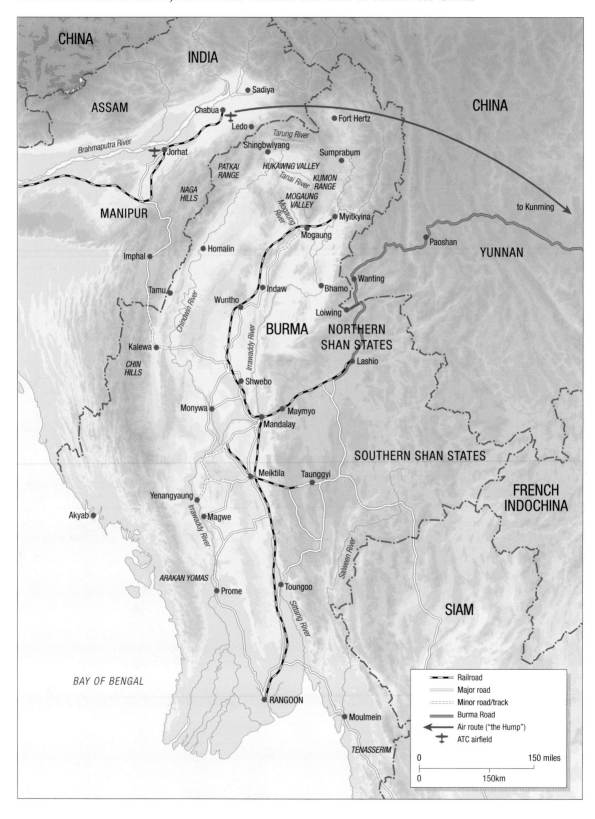

CHINA

INDIA

ASSAM

Sadiya

Chabua

Ledo

Tarung River

Fort Hertz

CHINA

Brahmaputra River

Jorhat

Shingbwiyang

Sumprabum

PATKAI RANGE

HUKAWNG VALLEY

KUMON RANGE

Tanai River

NAGA HILLS

MOGAUNG VALLEY

MANIPUR

Mogaung River

Myitkyina

to Kunming

Mogaung

Paoshan

YUNNAN

Homalin

Imphal

Indaw

Bhamo

Wanting

Tamu

Wuntho

Loiwing

Chindwin River

BURMA

NORTHERN SHAN STATES

Kalewa

Irrawaddy River

CHIN HILLS

Shwebo

Lashio

Monywa

Maymyo

Mandalay

Meiktila

Taunggyi

SOUTHERN SHAN STATES

Yenangyaung

FRENCH INDOCHINA

Akyab

Irrawaddy River

Magwe

Salween River

ARAKAN YOMAS

Prome

Toungoo

SIAM

Sittang River

BAY OF BENGAL

	Railroad
	Major road
	Minor road/track
	Burma Road
	Air route ("the Hump")
	ATC airfield

RANGOON

Moulmein

TENASSERIM

0   150 miles

0   150km

ORIGINS OF THE CAMPAIGN

THE JAPANESE OCCUPATION OF BURMA

Burma's occupation was an integral part of Japanese planning for both strategic and economic reasons. Burma not only provided large quantities of rice and oil, but she was also an important component in Japan's plans to conquer India, forming the land link connecting India and Malaya. If Burma could be occupied after the conquest of Britain's Far East military bastions – Hong Kong, Malaya, and Singapore – then an overland offensive into Britain's "jewel in the crown" might be possible.

The Japanese invasion of Burma from the eastern frontiers of Thailand started within a week of Pearl Harbor when elements of the Imperial Japanese Army (IJA) captured Victoria Point on the southern tip of Burma. By mid-January 1942, the Japanese had seized airfields from which to support operations in Burma at Mergui, Victoria Point, and Tavoy in Tenasserim, the strip of Burma in the Kra Isthmus. The IJA Fifteenth Army, consisting of the 33d and 55th divisions, waited along the Thai border until operations in Malaya neared completion, to begin their major Burmese invasion on January 20. The Japanese principal objectives were Rangoon, Burma's capital and major port; the communication centers of Prome and Toungoo; the Yenangyaung oilfields; and Mandalay, Central Burma's major city.

On April 18 and 19, the entire 33d Division broke the British defensive positions at Yenangyaung and drove into the oilfields. The British managed to destroy the facilities, which produced over a million gallons of gasoline daily. To their glee, the inglorious Allied retreat throughout all of Burma had commenced. The ensuing capture of the entire country by IJA forces left both India and China in dire straits. The Japanese landed troops on both sides of the Chindwin River on April 27 with orders to move northward to try to cut the Kalewa–Tamu route of British retreat towards the northeastern Indian

A truck convoy winds its way along a section of the Burma Road in southwestern China, aptly called "Twenty-Three Curves" after the number of hairpin bends. In order to get trucks from India to China, the Ledo Road, along with gasoline and water pipelines, would need to be constructed just behind Stilwell's offensive in northern Burma's Hukawng and Mogaung valleys. This would lead to the eventual capture of Myitkyina and a link-up with the Burma Road. (USAMHI)

Japanese infantry, with their officers mounted, advance into southeastern Burma across the Thai frontier as part of the effort to capture Rangoon. Elements of the 143d Infantry Regiment of the 55th Division reached Victoria Point on December 16, 1941 unopposed. Here, Burmese natives passively observe the invasion commencing. (USAMHI)

Both the Japanese and the Allies used elephants to help carry supply loads and weapons. Surprisingly, an elephant could not carry much more than a mule or a horse, but its remarkable talent lay in moving heavy logs for bridge building. Here a Japanese soldier leads an oozie (a Burmese elephant handler) atop his charge on an almost dry riverbed. Note that the Japanese soldier is walking barefoot, trying to preserve the longevity of his boots, since resupply was becoming more and more difficult in the face of Stilwell's continuing offensive. It is estimated that over 4,000 Burmese elephants died during the war. (USAMHI)

province of Assam. A divided Japanese high command now rejected a plan (considering it logistically impractical) to advance through northern Burma's Hukawng Valley and then descend on Assam by marching through the Brahmaputra Valley from Ledo. The conquest of Burma was now complete; Japanese losses totaled 4,597 killed and wounded.

Additionally, "the only means for supplies to reach [China], except across the long land frontier with Russia, was through Rangoon whence there was a good railroad link via Mandalay with the Chinese frontier at Wanting. From there a rough, single lane, fair-weather track to Kunming and Chungking had been hacked out in the autumn of 1938 by an army of 200,000 laborers. This was the famous Burma Road. No other artery of communication carried so little and yet exerted such a great influence on the strategy of the Second World War" (Callahan 1978, p. 25). If Rangoon were occupied and the Burma Road severed by the Japanese, then the Allies would need a more pragmatic way to supply Chiang Kai-shek's forces combating the IJA in their near decade-long conflict on the Asian land mass. Compelling China's capitulation by destroying all of its supply lines would enable the IJA to redistribute its massive Asian mainland forces to other Pacific war zones, possibly halting the nascent Allied plans to recapture their lost territory.

THE ALLIES IN BURMA

Britain needed to maintain a strong presence in Burma to protect the vital industrial areas situated in northeast India, the Burma Road, and the airfields in southern Burma near the Thai border. However, the only British troops available in Burma at the onset of hostilities were the 1st Burma Division and the 13th Indian Brigade. Fearing a Japanese attack from Thailand, the British high command sent the 16th and 48th Indian brigades and the rest of the 17th Indian Division to bolster the defenses. Ironically, all of these formations were lacking in jungle training, with the 17th Indian Division having been previously trained for the North African desert. The latter was of better quality than the 1st Burma Division, which was ordered to hold the line of the Salween River and cover Rangoon.

The Japanese advance in southeast Burma had been swift, passing the Salween and Bilin river lines, and now the defensive positions along the Sittang River were near to collapse. An order to withdraw across the Sittang was issued for February 23, 1942; however, a miscommunication resulted in the premature destruction of the bridge, with many British–Indian troops stranded on the eastern side of the river. Rangoon, the main British base in Burma, was in jeopardy. General Sir Harold Alexander arrived there on March 5 to assume command of the Burma Army after its previous commander was sacked. Assessing the military situation as untenable, Alexander gave the order for the British garrison at Rangoon to move out for Prome in Central Burma on March 6, setting fire to as many important buildings as possible the next day. The Japanese entered the city on March 8.

Three Chinese armies (each equivalent to a British division) – the Fifth, Sixth, and Sixty-Sixth – had been moved into Burma from the Chinese province of Yunnan between February and April to help stem the surging Japanese tide. Chiang Kai-shek had put the American general Joseph W. Stilwell, who had been sent to China by President Franklin Roosevelt, in independent command of these forces when he arrived at Lashio on March 14, 1942 (following an initial meeting with the Generalissimo on March 6 at Maymyo). Later in March, Alexander was asked to command all the Chinese

Indian troops take up defensive positions on the Sittang River, awaiting the Japanese assault. On the night of February 22/23, 1942, a controversial order was given, based on a miscommunication, to blow up the great bridge across the river. The line of retreat of the British and Indian troops still on the eastern side of the river was thus severed. (NARA RG 208-AA-160-B-1)

Lieutenant-General Joseph W. Stilwell (left) and General Sir Archibald P. Wavell meet in New Delhi, India in October 1942. The initial command structure in the China-Burma-India (CBI) theater produced a sharp contrast and clash of wills between two of the principal Allied leaders, which led to a political and diplomatic rift. Wavell, as C-in-C India, did not share Stilwell's strategic optimism for a counteroffensive in Burma so soon after the recent rout. (USAMHI)

troops in Burma in the interest of unity, to which Stilwell assented. Stilwell was contemplating a counteroffensive; however, that plan disintegrated when the Chinese troops failed to stop the Japanese at Toungoo after a ten-day stand. One of Alexander's primary roles was to defend the road from Mandalay to Lashio, the major link with China, as well as Mandalay and the Yenangyaung oilfields. Alexander realized there was no chance of stopping the Japanese with his forces both weakened and now unfit for combat. His hope was to retard the complete capitulation of Burma to the Japanese with his British and Indian forces, which comprised the remnants of the 17th Indian and the 1st Burma divisions along with the 7th Armoured Brigade (Burcorps), now under Lieutenant-General William J. Slim as of March 19. The Allies could no longer hold a defensive line at Prome against the Japanese who attacked about midnight on April 1/2, forcing a withdrawal from that position on April 2. Simultaneously, the Japanese were also advancing northward from Rangoon to Mandalay. On April 3, Slim outlined his plans to deny to the enemy the oilfields at Yenangyaung further north up the Irrawaddy River from Prome. However, they ultimately fell to the Japanese on April 18/19.

After Wavell had ordered Alexander to prepare for a withdrawal from Burma, the majority of the remaining British troops that had amassed in Mandalay began crossing the Irrawaddy River on the night of April 25/26 for their retreat to the Chindwin River and Assam. On April 26, Alexander decided that his main objective must be the defense of India. The withdrawal of as much as possible of the Burma Army to India for reorganization was the paramount goal. Alexander's forces had already begun their withdrawal in the direction of Kalewa, which Wavell was going to stock with supplies to arrive between May 6 and 12, just prior to the monsoon setting in. The last of the British troops left Burma on May 20, as IV Corps assumed operational command of all units from Burma; Alexander's command came to an end

A C-46 Commando of the Air Transport Command (ATC) flies the treacherous "Hump" over the snow-capped Himalayan foothills on a path from the air depots of Assam to Yunnan in southwestern China. After the initial failure of supply planes to reach China from India, Brigadier William D. Old, the head of ATC, personally flew a plane and made it through, indicating that the Japanese were not able to put up a constant stream of fighter aircraft to completely interdict the route. (NARA RG-208-AA-Q-41)

The Japanese advance through Burma, January to May 1942

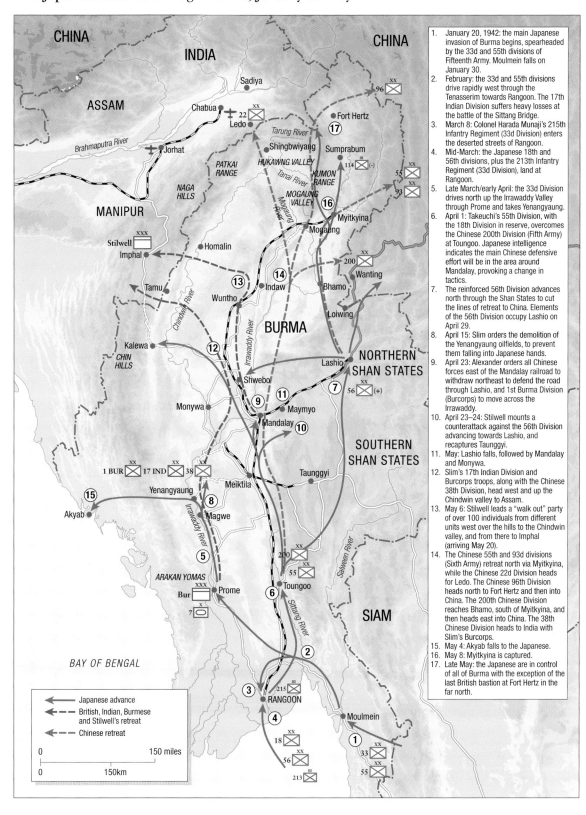

1. January 20, 1942: the main Japanese invasion of Burma begins, spearheaded by the 33d and 55th divisions of Fifteenth Army. Moulmein falls on January 30.
2. February: the 33d and 55th divisions drive rapidly west through the Tenasserim towards Rangoon. The 17th Indian Division suffers heavy losses at the battle of the Sittang Bridge.
3. March 8: Colonel Harada Munaji's 215th Infantry Regiment (33d Division) enters the deserted streets of Rangoon.
4. Mid-March: the Japanese 18th and 56th divisions, plus the 213th Infantry Regiment (33d Division), land at Rangoon.
5. Late March/early April: the 33d Division drives north up the Irrawaddy Valley through Prome and takes Yenangyaung.
6. April 1: Takeuchi's 55th Division, with the 18th Division in reserve, overcomes the Chinese 200th Division (Fifth Army) at Toungoo. Japanese intelligence indicates the main Chinese defensive effort will be in the area around Mandalay, provoking a change in tactics.
7. The reinforced 56th Division advances north through the Shan States to cut the lines of retreat to China. Elements of the 56th Division occupy Lashio on April 29.
8. April 15: Slim orders the demolition of the Yenangyaung oilfields, to prevent them falling into Japanese hands.
9. April 23: Alexander orders all Chinese forces east of the Mandalay railroad to withdraw northeast to defend the road through Lashio, and 1st Burma Division (Burcorps) to move across the Irrawaddy.
10. April 23–24: Stilwell mounts a counterattack against the 56th Division advancing towards Lashio, and recaptures Taunggyi.
11. May: Lashio falls, followed by Mandalay and Monywa.
12. Slim's 17th Indian Division and Burcorps troops, along with the Chinese 38th Division, head west and up the Chindwin valley to Assam.
13. May 6: Stilwell leads a "walk out" party of over 100 individuals from different units west over the hills to the Chindwin valley, and from there to Imphal (arriving May 20).
14. The Chinese 55th and 93d divisions (Sixth Army) retreat north via Myitkyina, while the Chinese 22d Division heads for Ledo. The Chinese 96th Division heads north to Fort Hertz and then into China. The 200th Chinese Division reaches Bhamo, south of Myitkyina, and then heads east into China. The 38th Chinese Division heads to India with Slim's Burcorps.
15. May 4: Akyab falls to the Japanese.
16. May 8: Myitkyina is captured.
17. Late May: the Japanese are in control of all of Burma with the exception of the last British bastion at Fort Hertz in the far north.

An IJA pilot climbs into his Ki-43 in a mission to interdict Allied transport planes bound for southwestern China in the summer of 1942. Elements of the Imperial Japanese Army Air Force (IJAAF) 5th Air Division, which contained the 50th and 77th Fighter Sentai in its 4th Air Brigade and the 64th Fighter Sentai in the 7th Air Brigade, operated from the airfield complex at Myitkyina. A *sentai* was the equivalent of an American squadron. The Ki-43 was considered the IJA's best fighter. (USAMHI)

A wrecked American ATC transport plane shot down flying "the Hump," and contributing to the term "the Aluminum Trail," referring to the wreckages that dotted the Burmese landscape. As the ATC began cobbling together an air fleet by September 1942 with daily lifts of over 400 tons of supplies delivered to China, the Myitkyina-based Japanese air arm was waiting for the end of the monsoon season to contest the "Hump" route by launching the 50th Sentai in Operation *Tsuzigiri* (Street Murder). It became obvious to the Allied high command that Myitkyina would have to be captured to completely remove this continued air threat. (USAMHI)

after a 1,000-mile retreat, the longest withdrawal ever for a British army, taking over 3½ months. The first heavy rains of the monsoon fell on May 12; thus, Alexander had evacuated Burma by the slimmest of margins, since an additional week of fighting east of the Chindwin could have spelled disaster for the Burma Army. The British and Indian forces in Burma suffered 10,036 casualties, of whom 3,670 were killed and wounded and the remaining 6,366 missing.

Chiang's ground and American volunteer air forces combating the Japanese were now wholly isolated from resupply by both sea through Rangoon and overland across the Burma Road, and had to rely solely on a treacherous, mountainous air route over the Himalayas ("the Hump") from the air depots in India's northeastern provinces of Assam and Manipur to the Chinese southwestern provinces of Kunming and Yunnan. Flying over such terrain in rough weather, and at times in unreliable aircraft, contributed to the danger.

Myitkyina, the traditional capital of northern Burma, is located at the junction of the Mogaung and Irrawaddy valleys and lies at the southern tip of the Himalayas. Due to the ubiquitous threat of the IJAAF's single-engined Ki-43 *Hayabusa* (Peregrine Falcon) or "Oscar" and two-seated Ki-45 *Toryu* (Dragon Killer) or "Nick" fighters stationed at the Myitkyina airfield complex, Allied transport aircraft had to fly far to the north, then swing south to Kunming and Yunnan. However, using the more northerly route to avoid these fighters dramatically increased the fuel consumption of the ATC transports while also reducing their cargo payload. Furthermore, the air route itself was narrow and saturated with transports attempting to deliver the requisite tonnage to Chiang's forces. In a nutshell, this air-supply nightmare would persist as long as Myitkyina remained in Japanese hands.

CHRONOLOGY

1943

October 5	Lieutenant-General Sun Li-jen, commander of the Chinese 38th Division, receives orders to send his 112th Infantry Regiment forward in advance of the Ledo Road construction crews in order to shield them.
October 24	A company of the 2d Battalion, 56th Infantry Regiment, 18th Division of the IJA arrives in the Tarung–Tanai Hka area of the Hukawng Valley on reconnaissance, and constructs defensive outposts in and around Ningbyen.
October 30	The Chinese clash with the Japanese outpost on the Tarung Hka at Sharaw Ga.
Early November	The remainder of the Japanese 2d Battalion, 56th Infantry Regiment is sent to the forward outpost positions.
Mid-December	To combat the three battalions of the Chinese 112th Infantry Regiment, 38th Division that have been sent forward into the northern end of the Hukawng Valley, elements of the IJA 55th and 56th Infantry regiments of the 18th Division reinforce the forward Japanese outposts holding the line of the Tarung Hka and Tanai Hka near the village of Yupbang Ga, and encircle the Chinese.
December 21	Following the Cairo Conference (codenamed "Sextant"), Stilwell arrives at the front to find the advance already a month behind schedule as the Japanese continue to hold their line of fortified outposts at Yupbang Ga, where the Ledo Road will cross the Tarung. Brigadier-General Haydon L. Boatner (Stilwell's deputy in the Chinese Army in India, CAI) and Lieutenant-General Sun Li-jen have been unable to break the Chinese 112th Infantry Regiment's encirclement.
December 24–25	Stilwell personally directs companies from the 1st Battalion, 114th Infantry Regiment, Chinese 38th Division against Japanese reinforced positions with heavy machine guns surrounding Sun's 112th Infantry Regiment at Yupbang Ga.

1944

February 24–March 4	First mission of the 5307th Composite Unit (Provisional) culminates with their attack and block at Walawbum in the southern Hukawng Valley.
March 28–29	The 1st Battalion of the 5307th attacks the Japanese and establishes a roadblock just to the south of Shaduzup in the northern Mogaung Valley.

March 23–April 7	The 2d Battalion of the 5307th attacks the Japanese at Inkangahtawng, between Shaduzup and Kamaing; the 2d and 3d battalions hastily retreat east to Nhpum Ga and Hsamshingyang respectively, where a siege of the Marauders by Lieutenant-General Tanaka Shinichi's infantry ensues at the former site until April 7.
April 28–May 16	H, K, and M forces of the 5307th trek through the eastern part of the Kumon Range and arrive at Namkwi, just to the north of the main Myitkyina airfield west of the town.
May 17	H Force, under Colonel Hunter, with the 1st Battalion of the 5307th and the 150th Infantry Regiment of the Chinese 50th Division, captures the airfield to the west of Myitkyina town in a surprise morning attack.
June 2–25	Brigadier Michael Calvert's 77th Indian Infantry Brigade of Special Force (3rd Indian Division) attacks the outlying village entrenchments and then the town of Mogaung in a savage, conventional battle not suited to Major-General Orde Wingate's original Chindit doctrine.
May 17–August 3	Defense of the western Myitkyina airstrip and the protracted siege of Myitkyina town.
August 3	Myitkyina town is captured by a Sino-American force after the Japanese retreat leaving a rearguard of 200 wounded and debilitated soldiers.
October 2	One of the two pipelines from the Indian refineries via Ledo to Myitkyina enters operation.
September 19	Precipitated by the Japanese offensive Operation *Ichigo* (No. 1), Roosevelt and Chief of Staff George C. Marshall want Stilwell to take over all the Chinese armies in China. However, Generalissimo Chiang Kai-shek decides that Stilwell must be dismissed, in large part due to the struggle to control the Lend-Lease supplies.
October 18	Roosevelt agrees to Chiang Kai-shek's request for an immediate recall of Stilwell, which is relayed by Marshall to Stilwell the next day.
October 24	The Ledo Road nears completion.

1945

January 28	The Ledo Road reaches the Burma Road at Mong Yu and the first truck convoy enters the Chinese town of Wanting in Yunnan Province. Chiang Kai-shek renames the Ledo and Burma Road the "Stilwell Road."

OPPOSING COMMANDERS

JAPANESE COMMANDERS

Mutaguchi Renya initially commanded the 18th Division during the Burma campaign. He was described as a "heavy-bodied, bullet-headed officer with hard eyes and thick lips who fiercely overrode the intractable problem of supply and whose wrath was so feared by his staff that they did not press their doubts" (Tuchman 1970, p. 438). Earlier in his career, Mutaguchi was present at Japan's capture of Peking. When not demonstrating extreme condescension towards his seemingly inept Chinese opponents, Mutaguchi ridiculed his other vanquished enemy, the British, whom he swiftly defeated at Singapore in mid-February 1942 leading the 18th Division as part of Yamashita's Twenty-Fifth Army.

Following the occupation of Rangoon in early March 1942, elements of his 18th Division took part in the invasion of the Andaman Islands. His other battalions reached Rangoon via a convoy from Singapore on March 25 and would ultimately be tasked with cutting the Burma Road immediately east of Mandalay. In May 1942, the 18th Division was to move on and occupy Lashio and then clear the remaining Chinese forces in the Shan States south of the Burma Road. For logistical, terrain, and climatic reasons, Mutaguchi, among others, was not initially in favor of a Japanese invasion of Assam in 1942/43. The official Japanese policy for Burma for the dry weather of 1942/43 would remain defensive: the 18th Division would garrison northern Burma, with divisional HQ at Myitkyina, and alert to any threat to the Fifteenth Army's lines of communication.

In March 1943, Mutaguchi was promoted to command the Fifteenth Army when Lieutenant-General Iida Shojiro was reassigned to the General Defense Command in Japan. In the spring of 1943, he was certain that he had to concentrate his attack against India. The headquarters of IJA Fifteenth Army decided that an offensive–defensive strategy was sounder and more economical; after Longcloth, the HQ had concluded that the British, having evolved new tactics, might repeat the operation on a larger scale in conjunction with a major

Lieutenant-General Mutaguchi Renya served in China as a regimental commander in the 18th Division. During Yamashita's conquest of Malaya and Singapore, Mutaguchi led the 18th Division down the Malay Peninsula's east coast and crossed the Johore Strait to participate in the capture of Singapore in February 1942. He then commanded the 18th Division in Burma until March 1943, when he was promoted to command the Fifteenth Army. (USAMHI)

offensive. From April through the summer of 1943, Mutaguchi planned a three-division attack into India: the 33d Division under Lieutenant-General Yanagida Motoso was to advance towards Imphal from the south against the 17th Indian Division; the 15th Division under Lieutenant-General Yamauchi Masafumi was to attack Imphal in two prongs from the east; and, most significantly, the 31st Division under Lieutenant-General Sato Kotoku was to advance to Dimapur, the huge (11-mile long and 1-mile wide) supply base which provided for the whole of Slim's Eastern Army. Mutaguchi intended that as soon as Kohima and Dimapur were captured, his victorious forces, accompanied by the Indian National Army and its leader, Subhas Chandra Bose, would advance into Bengal where the subjugated Indian populace would mount an internal insurrection against British rule and support his triumphant "March on Delhi."

It is seldom mentioned that Mutaguchi almost accomplished his strategic aim. If success had come to Mutaguchi's Operation *U-Go* of March–June 1944, British, Chinese, and American forces operating in Burma would have seen all contact with the west severed. An incorrect logistic and supply decision by this otherwise outstanding Japanese commander, along with the selfless bravery of Indian and British troops, thwarted *U-Go*. His idea of commencing the offensive with only one month's rations and supplies, in anticipation of capturing the stores at Dimapur, became a significant factor in its ultimate failure. The Japanese had no equivalent of the American and British air supply capabilities to troops on the ground in fortified positions (e.g. Wingate's strongholds such as "White City") or on the move in the jungles and hills of Burma.

Japanese generals of the Burma Area Army in late 1943. Lieutenant-General Mutaguchi, in command of the Fifteenth Army for Operation *U-Go*, is seated in the middle of the first row, while Lieutenant-General Tanaka, 18th Division commander, is seated second from the left in the same row. (NARA 2194532)

Kawabe Masakazu had held the position of Chief of Staff, Japanese Expeditionary Force in China, for a long interval. At the time of the outbreak of the China Incident in 1937, both Kawabe and Mutaguchi were serving in north China, the former as a brigade commander and the latter as a regimental commander. On March 27, 1943 Burma Area Army Headquarters was established, under the command of Kawabe; its Fifteenth Army was tasked with defending central and northern Burma, and the 55th Division defended Arakan. Kawabe reported to General Count Terauchi Hisaichi, commander of the Southern Army, based in Saigon. Kawabe's primary task was Burma's defense, but he also had charge of planning Japanese offensive operations across the Chindwin frontier into Assam. Kawabe thought that Mutaguchi's plan was far too ambitious and that he would take too many risks, as he did not take into account the improved fighting value of the British forces in Assam. Kawabe wanted an offensive across the Chindwin and Indian frontier to gain the general line of Kohima–Imphal and advance no further; however, Mutaguchi wanted to take his army into the Brahmaputra Valley and eventually, to a "March on Delhi," which was beyond the limit of Kawabe's instructions.

ALLIED COMMANDERS

Joseph W. Stilwell graduated from West Point in 1904 and served as an infantry second lieutenant in the Philippines during the Moro insurrection, as a chief intelligence officer for General Pershing's St Mihiel offensive, and two years later as the Army's initial Intelligence Division's Chinese language officer in Peking. While there, Stilwell was an informal engineering adviser

Lieutenant-General Tanaka Shinichi served in Manchuria from 1931 to 1932, and then held a series of staff positions prior to a major military planning role for the Pacific War. Due to political disfavor in Tokyo, Tanaka became the commanding officer of the 18th Division in northern Burma in March 1943 after Mutaguchi's promotion to lead Fifteenth Army. After the fall of Myitkyina and the near destruction of the 18th Division, Tanaka was appointed chief of staff of the Burma Area Army. (USAMHI)

Stilwell, who preferred being at the front with his troops rather than back in India or at Chunking in China, rides in a short column of jeeps through a shallow stream in Burma while his force campaigns down the Hukawng and Mogaung valleys. He wears his iconic campaign hat and carries his trademark M1 carbine rifle. (USAMHI)

for a road-building project in a remote area of China, where he absorbed all aspects of Chinese culture and language, and developed a keen respect for the hard-driving work ethic of the Chinese peasant laborer. In 1924, during the first of two additional tours in China, he commanded a battalion of the 15th Infantry Regiment, stationed at Tientsin, where he initially met his mentor, George C. Marshall.

In 1926, during a state of civil war involving many factions, Major Stilwell was sent into the countryside to gather first-hand information about the extent of the unrest. By 1929, he was on his way to becoming a recognized expert on China in the eyes of his United States Army peers and superiors.

After four years of teaching infantry tactics at Fort Benning, as Marshall's deputy, and earning the moniker "Vinegar Joe" for his acerbic commentary and salty language, Colonel Stilwell was appointed military attaché to China in July 1935. Shortly after the Pearl Harbor attack, Stilwell was ordered to Washington, where he expected to be given a command tasked with invading North Africa. However, US Army Chief of Staff Marshall and Secretary of War Henry L. Stimson wanted Stilwell to be the CBI theater commander and Chiang Kai-shek's deputy, among other Lend-Lease supply roles, since he was fluent in Chinese and embodied strategic vision and tactical inventiveness, and, above all, was an excellent trainer of both American and Chinese soldiers.

With the general collapse of the entire Allied position in late April 1942, Stilwell started his "Walkout" with 114 others in his party westwards towards India. By May 13, after the 140-mile trek from Indaw to Assam, without any losses, a war reporter observing the general coming out of the jungle stated that he looked "like the wrath of God and cursing like a fallen angel" (Mortimer 2013, p. 3).

Frank D. Merrill graduated from West Point in 1929 in the same class as his future deputy, Charles N. Hunter. He served as a Japanese-language officer in the Philippines and was transferred to Burma after Pearl Harbor to liaise with the British. In that role, he pinpointed for Stilwell the failures of the 1942 campaign as, "no plan, no reconnaissance, no security, no intelligence, no prisoners in contrast to the Japanese who had excellent communication, great aggressiveness and high mobility" (quoted in Tuchman 1970, p. 272). Stilwell eventually received the 5307th Composite Unit (Provisional), being trained by Wingate and commanded by Colonel Charles Hunter; however, the command of Galahad (the 5307th's codename) for the Sino-American invasion of northern Burma for 1943–44 was given to Merrill, who now became a brigadier-general. At times during the offensive, Merrill was so weak from his heart ailments that he had to be ordered back to a Ledo hospital.

Merrill confers with two of his Nisei Marauder interpreters from the 3d Battalion, Staff Sergeant L. Herb Miyazaki and Staff Sergeant R. Akiji Yokimura, at Hsamshingyang in late March 1944. These Marauders would often approach close to Japanese lines or tap into enemy field communications, relaying any intelligence gleaned back to the battalion officers and Merrill. (NARA 559282 MM 140)

Brigadier-General Lewis Pick (left), head of the Ledo Road and pipeline construction project, views progress with Admiral Lord Louis Mountbatten, commander South East Asia Command (SEAC), together with other British officers, at Ledo on April 7, 1944. (NARA 111-SC-262504)

Lewis Pick, before arriving in the CBI theater as a colonel, had been a civil engineer of the Missouri River Division and had drawn up the Pick Plan of Missouri River flood control. On October 17, 1943 Pick assumed complete command of the Ledo Road project. At the extreme northeastern end of the vital railway line in Assam, construction of the Ledo Road was resumed as the end of the rains and the gradual drying of the ground permitted work to begin. To aid the work on "Pick's Pike," he would command five individual US Army engineer battalions and a quartermaster regiment. From the end of October 1943 to the end of November, the lead bulldozer on the project advanced 22 miles to mile marker 82.35 from Ledo. Anticipating that the road would soon be through the mountain barrier of the Hukawng Valley, Colonel Pick sent 19 men ahead to the village of Shingbwiyang (mile 103 from Ledo) on the southern end of the Patkai Range to establish a supply depot for the first truck convoy. At Shingbwiyang, Pick's construction units would be roughly one-third of the way from Ledo to Myitkyina and the now Japanese-controlled Burma Road.

Sun Li-jen, commander of the Chinese 38th Division, received his military education at the Virginia Military Institute and spoke English well. He was on occasion given British troops to command in 1942, and earned their respect. British commanders found him an able tactician, alert, aggressive and cool in battle. He was perhaps the outstanding man among the Chinese leaders and certainly the most competent, also earning the respect of both Stilwell and Slim.

Liao Yao-hsiang was a graduate of St Cyr in France. During the defeat in late March 1942, Stilwell was critical of the tardiness of his Chinese 22d Division's attack and caustically described him in his diary as "a colorless bird, who talked a lot at high speed without saying anything" (quoted in Tuchman 1970, p. 277). However, at the Ramgarh training facility, he faithfully complied with all training directives, and as a result his division became as good as the 38th, which had a long start ahead of him. During the campaign of 1943–44, he was judged to be "a good field soldier, courageous and determined" and a

Stilwell (center) goes over plans with Lieutenant-General Sun (left, commander 38th Division) and Lieutenant-General Liao (commander 22d Division) during the advance down the Hukawng Valley in early 1944. (USAMHI)

"capable commander" (quoted in Romanus and Sunderland 1970, p. 34). However, it became apparent that obedience to orders depended in the end on fear of sanctions, and Sun and Liao were well aware that it was from Chiang Kai-shek, not Stilwell, that sanctions would flow.

Orde C. Wingate was posted with the Royal Garrison Artillery in 1923 after graduating from the Royal Military Academy, Woolwich. Learning Arabic and using family connections, Wingate was posted to the Sudan Defence Force (SDF) and led an infantry company (Idara) of 375 men near the Eritrean border from 1928 to 1933. In that isolated backwater, Wingate developed military principles about small groups of soldiers surviving in a desolate, inhospitable environment. Training, fitness, and fieldcraft became his credos, which would enable his troops to remain afar from their garrison without lines of communication. Marching his company 500 miles into remote areas of eastern Sudan, Wingate experimented with ground-to-air control with RAF Squadron 47 (B), heralding this emerging tactic for future commands.

In September 1936, Wingate was posted as an intelligence officer (GSO "I") with the 5th Division in Palestine. During the Arab Revolt in 1937 and 1938, General Archibald Wavell, GOC, Palestine, accepted Wingate's plan to form small units of British soldiers and Jewish paramilitary volunteers – Special Night Squads (SNS) – to be used offensively against the Arab insurgents, who were sabotaging the Iraq Petroleum Company's pipeline to Haifa. A patron-protégée relationship was forged between Wavell and Wingate, the latter receiving the Distinguished Service Order (DSO) for his nocturnal ambushes throughout the summer of 1938, which dramatically reduced the number of times that the pipeline was breached.

In September 1940, Wavell, now C-in-C, Middle East, asked for Wingate to be sent to Africa "to fan into flame the embers of revolt that had smouldered in parts of the Abyssinian highlands ever since the Italian occupation" (quoted in Diamond 2012, p. 19). Wingate arrived in Khartoum and developed a force of Ethiopian rebels as well as some Sudanese regular

Major-General Orde Wingate with Brigadier Michael Calvert (right) and RAF Wing Commander Robert Thompson at "White City," a motor road and railway block and stronghold at the village of Henu, during Operation Thursday in March 1944. By interdicting road and rail traffic to the north, Calvert and his 77th Indian Infantry Brigade significantly interdicted the flow of supplies to Tanaka's 18th Division troops in the Hukawng and Mogaung valleys at a time when Stilwell's offensive was continuing strongly. (USAMHI)

troops to administer "shock therapy" to the Italians in Ethiopia's Gojjam Province, eventually defeating them in May 1941. In Ethiopia, Wingate's expedition into the Gojjam with Gideon Force became a blueprint for his long-range penetration (LRP) concept.

During the British setbacks in fighting the Japanese in Burma, in early 1942, General Archibald Wavell, now C-in-C, India, summoned Colonel Wingate to Burma to join his staff to help stem the unstoppable Japanese advance. In April 1942, Wingate was sent to Maymyo to take command of guerrilla operations in Burma. There, Wingate met Major Michael Calvert at the Bush Warfare School and was impressed by his fighting zeal and willingness to lead commando-style assaults against the Japanese.

Michael Calvert had led a detachment of Royal Engineers during the ill-fated Norwegian campaign. After transferring to the prewar Pacific, he trained commandos in demolitions in both Hong Kong and Australia, eventually leading to a command position at the Bush Warfare School. However, the deteriorating situation impeded Wingate's ability to direct Calvert's unit since the Japanese had overrun that section of Burma in strength. Thus, Wingate returned to Delhi at the end of April 1942 and wrote a memorandum to Wavell on LRP, which would "mushroom" into Operation Longcloth in February 1943 under the now field marshal's penchant for unorthodox tactics.

William J. Slim lacked formal military education, but after having joined the Birmingham University Officers' Training Corps, he was commissioned as a temporary second lieutenant into the Royal Warwickshire Regiment in 1914 and fought at Gallipoli, where he was wounded. After rejoining his regiment in Mesopotamia in 1916, he was again wounded in combat and won an MC for his exploits in Mesopotamia. Most of his life between the wars was spent with the Gurkhas. Earlier in 1940–41, he fought with distinction in Abyssinia, Syria, Iraq, and Persia. In March 1942, Alexander gave him command of Burma Corps (Burcorps) as an acting lieutenant-general. He led his corps out of Burma to India with distinction. After the failed Arakan Campaign of 1943, Slim was promoted to command the new Fourteenth Army formed from the various corps in India. The Fourteenth Army decisively destroyed Mutaguchi's Fifteenth Army in its "March on Delhi" in the Naga Hills and Manipur between March and July 1944.

OPPOSING FORCES

JAPANESE FORCES

The Japanese Fifteenth Army in Burma was typified by the 18th Division, first under Mutaguchi and then Tanaka. The IJA prepared late for war in tropical training environments. At the start of 1941, Lieutenant-Colonel Tsuji Masanobu, a highly regarded staff officer at Twenty-Fifth Army headquarters, joined the IJA's jungle warfare school on the island of Formosa as its commander. Practical modes for jungle combat were perfected, including issuing headbands to soldiers to keep the sweat from pouring into their eyes while aiming their rifles; utilizing lighter weapons and loads for the hot, steamy climate; and incorporating the terrain as an added dimension, such as getting off trails or jungle tracks and using the verdant foliage to conceal flanking movements around the enemy. Tsuji's researchers prepared a pamphlet, *Read This Alone and the War Can Be Won*, which was approved by the Imperial Japanese Headquarters for wide dissemination among IJA troops. Stilwell, and more convincingly Wingate, tried to imbue their troops with these Japanese jungle lessons at Ramgarh and Deogarh, respectively.

The 18th Division's three regiments were garrisoned throughout northern Burma, and thus fought the Chindits during both the 1943 and 1944 campaigns as well as contesting Stilwell's Sino-American advance down the Hukawng and Mogaung valleys towards Myitkyina, which began in the late autumn of 1943. The 18th Division, during Operation Longcloth, was one of the best divisions in the IJA and garrisoned the area through which Wingate's columns moved. The men of this division were from the Nagasaki and Fukuoka areas of Kyushu, noted for producing a robust and bellicose warrior. The division's troops possessed élan, having seen heavy fighting in China.

By 1941, the 18th Division had accumulated as much operational experience as most Anglo-American divisions would acquire in the entire war.

This division had taken part in the Shanghai–Nanking campaign of 1937, with Mutaguchi as a regimental commander, and other campaigns in China. The vigor of the 18th Division had been shown in the jungle blitzkrieg which had won Malaya for the Japanese between December 1941 and February 1942, as well as the rapid advance in Burma.

The Japanese did not just sit back and wait to be attacked. In the Hukawng Valley and the Indaw area, 18th Division battalions were split up into smaller units for active patrolling, since in essence the 55th and 56th Infantry regiments were forward outposts in the vastness of the Burmese jungle. Led by Colonel Koba Hiroshi, the 55th Infantry Regiment was responsible for the area west of the Zibyu Range, roughly from Homalin to Mawlaik. The regimental HQ was at Katha on the Irrawaddy River. Over 100 miles north of Myitkyina, the 2d Battalion of the 114th Infantry Regiment, stationed at Myitkyina, comprised a punitive force directed at the British-led Kachins at Sumprabum. This division of major 18th Division units meant that Japanese commanders would fight the American, Chinese, British, and Kachin forces in a piecemeal fashion rather than with an overwhelming concentration of force.

Horses carry Japanese artillery pieces broken down into smaller parts, along with ammunition boxes. The mountainous terrain and narrow trails made it extremely treacherous for pack animals with their heavy loads. (USAMHI)

The principal tactic for the Japanese infantryman was to close with the enemy, often by surprise and with the element of darkness, to impose maximum confusion. The infantry relied on light machine guns (LMGs) and heavy machine guns (HMGs), the latter in fortified outposts or prearranged ambushes due to a weight of over 120lb. A favorite fire support weapon, highly regarded by the Allied soldiers too, was the Type 89 grenade discharger, which could hurl a standard 19oz Type 91 grenade up to a maximum range of 175yd. When a Type 89 shell was used, even greater distances could be achieved; the Allies referred to this weapon incorrectly as a "knee mortar." This weapon inflicted an incredibly high percentage of casualties among Allied infantrymen and could be used much more easily in the jungle than traditional Japanese 70mm and 81mm mortars.

For the IJA, the role of artillery was to support the infantry; thus, the guns were lightweight, thereby sacrificing both range and ruggedness. The battalion gun platoon was equipped with two Type 92 70mm battalion guns with an effective range of 1,500yd and a maximum range of 3,000yd; these were often employed in a direct-fire role. Unlike comparable Allied guns, the Type 92 could be broken down and carried by its ten-man gun section along the Burmese jungle tracks and rugged mountain paths. Because of its versatility and mobility, the battalion gun was present in most infantry engagements. A limited number of tanks were used by the Japanese in Burma in contrast to earlier fighting in the Philippines, Malaya, and Singapore.

In mid-December 1943, elements of the 55th and 56th Infantry regiments of the 18th Division established forward outposts near the village of Yupbang Ga to combat the three battalions of the 112th Infantry Regiment of the

ATTACK ON "THE HUMP," OCTOBER 13, 1943 (PP. 22–23)

Japanese fighters (Ki-43-II "Oscars") are shown attacking C-47 ("Dakota") transports on "the Hump" on October 13, 1943 – the launch date of Operation *Tsujigiri* (Street Murder). This engagement took place c.100 miles south of Fort Hertz in northeast Burma. The fighters are from the 50th Sentai, stationed at Myitkyina some 150 miles south of Fort Hertz. Pilots of the 50th Sentai claimed to have downed three transports (a C-47, a C-46, and a C-87, the latter a cargo variant of the B-24 Liberator) on this date.

Flying "the Hump" was hazardous for the pilots and crews of the ATC, in their c.700-mile trek from air depots in India to their terminals at Yunnanyi and Kunming in southwestern China. Two spurs of the Himalaya Mountains sharply divide the three nations of India, Burma, and China. In early 1942 this barrier was crossed by nothing more than jungle trails. Banks of cumulus and cumulo-nimbus clouds could sometimes tower between 2,000 and 25,000ft, which could be deadly for pilots. In these clouds, turbulence with winds of 100–200mph would pile into the steep barren slopes and then bounce off them, creating updrafts over the ridges and downdrafts over the valleys. Transports caught in a downdraft could drop at a rate of 5,000ft per minute. Furthermore, the air route itself was narrow, and midair collisions between transports did occur.

In March 1943, the 50th Sentai was stationed at Meiktila in central Burma; however, after having been fully re-equipped with the Ki-43-II **(1)**, this Sentai moved to Myitkyina to interdict the "Hump" route. As of the autumn of 1943, the air defense of Burma was handed to the IJAAF's 5th Air Brigade, which contained, among others, the 50th and 64th sentais.

A single Allied cargo plane could carry approximately 4–5 tons,

and under optimum conditions could make one round trip per day. Losses over the route were heavy. In three years of operation, the ATC was to lose 468 planes, an average of 13 a month. Sometimes the crew was able to parachute to safety and be guided out by Kachin rescue teams organized by OSS agents in Burma. Others died in the jungle or were captured by the Japanese.

In December 1942, the ATC took over air supply of China from the Tenth Air Force, establishing its India–China Wing, ATC (ICWATC) as controlling headquarters. ICWATC also commanded 22nd, 28th, 29th, and 30th Transport groups, each with 3–4 squadrons along with the 64th and 443rd Troop Carrier groups with 4–5 squadrons each; all composed of C-47s **(2)**. In June 1943, ATC had 146 transports committed to the "Hump" route and by September of that year, the number of transports rose to 225 transports. ATC's goal was to replace all C-47s flying the "Hump" with larger, more powerful C-46s, but the first of these to reach the CBI proved to be so unreliable that they were returned to the US for repairs. The ATC would have to rely on C-47s well into 1944.

The Ki-43-II was a modification of the initial production model, the highly maneuverable Ki-43-I. The IJAAF's fighter sentais in Burma and China began converting to the Ki-43-II soon after it entered production. The 64th converted in December 1942, followed by the 50th in February–March 1943, the 25th Sentai in May and the 33d shortly thereafter. The Ki-43-II was fitted with two Ho-103 Type 1 12.7mm machine guns fitted in the forward fuselage and synchronized to fire through the propeller arc. The fighter was fitted with the more powerful 1,130hp Nakajima Ha-115 radial engine driving a three-bladed metal propeller.

Chinese 38th Division that were sent forward into the northern end of the Hukawng Valley to hold the line of the Tarung Hka and Tanai Hka. The Chinese battalions were soon cut off as the Japanese used their customary tactic of encirclement, causing Sun Li-jen's troops to become wholly reliant on air supply. The Japanese were impressed by the unexpected stubbornness of the Chinese troops fighting around Yupbang Ga, leading them to believe that Stilwell's Chinese force was far superior in both quality and quantity. Witnessing the Allied air supply drop made the Japanese realize that they had nothing remotely similar to that capability even while still in control of the overland lines of communication from Mandalay to Myitkyina.

A destroyed Japanese Type 95 Ke-Go light tank viewed from the rear, with a Burmese pagoda in the background. The armor on this four-man tank was only 4–14mm thick. It had one 37mm gun and two 7.7mm machine guns, one forward and one aft; however, the major drawback was that the commander had to operate the gun in addition to his normal duties, impeding its combat effectiveness. (USAMHI)

ALLIED FORCES

Both the Chinese 38th and 22d divisions fought in Burma during early 1942 prior to their eventual retreat, re-formation and retraining by Stilwell, America's foremost infantry instructor, at his troop-training center at Ramgarh, India. Ramgarh was officially opened in August 1942 with the 9,000 survivors of the Burma campaign that had escaped to Imphal in May 1942 as a nucleus, to be augmented by an additional 23,500 flown in from China on the "back-haul of empty U.S. aircraft after delivery of air cargoes to Yunnan" (Boatner 1971, p. 6). However, a large proportion of these Chinese troops were in the hospital – ragged and half-starved, as well as disease-ridden with malaria, amebic dysentery, and potentially fatal Naga sores. Getting appropriate medical treatment, vaccinations, and adequate nutrition, the average Chinese soldier gained over 20lb in the initial month at Ramgarh. Also, these soldiers received uniforms, helmets, and weapons, and eventually training in operating artillery, Bren carriers, and American M3 light tanks. Under a crash program using American instructors, the Chinese made remarkable progress. Slim noted: "Everywhere was Stilwell, urging, leading, driving" (quoted in Rooney 2005, p. 93). Sun Li-jen, commanding the 38th Division and Liao Yao-hsiang, the 22d Division commander, were the senior officers.

By the end of December 1942, 32,000 Chinese troops were in training at Ramgarh to create a two-division force (Chinese 38th and 22d divisions) along with three accompanying artillery regiments, and the 1st Provisional Tank Group comprising M3 light tanks and under the command of the American Colonel Rothwell H. Brown; many American NCOs served in the tanks, peaking at 29 officers and 222 enlisted men. The group had an integrated Sino-American staff, a Chinese vice-commander (Colonel Chao Chen-yu), and an American medium tank platoon in support. Colonel (later Brigadier-General) Haydon L. Boatner, who had Chinese language experience and had served in the US 15th Infantry Regiment at Tientsin, became chief of staff of the task force in training and, ultimately, the deputy commander of the *Chih Hui Pu*, or Chinese Army in India (CAI). At Ramgarh, Chinese officers were trained in tactics and how to react in combat conditions, much like that which occurred under Stilwell's tutelage at Fort Benning in the early 1930s. The recruits received "hands-on" training in the use of rifles, machine guns, mortars, antitank guns, and rocket launchers. Jungle warfare training was also implemented, and for artillery crews a six-week course in the use of pack artillery and howitzers with emphasis on jungle conditions.

In late August 1943, after the Quadrant Conference in Quebec, a call was sent from the War Department for a "hazardous mission." The mission's codename was Galahad, and a force of 3,000 troops would be raised in a month for a three-month mission that would cause approximately 85 percent casualties. Dated September 18, 1943, a memo describing the status of the recruitment of the "1688th Casual Detachment" was secretly disseminated:

> 960 jungle-trained officers and men from the Caribbean Defense Command;
> 970 jungle-trained officers and men from the Army Ground Forces;
> 674 battle-tested jungle troops from the South Pacific are being assembled at Noumea;
> General Macarthur was directed to furnish 274 battle-tested troops. He was able to secure only 55 volunteers meeting our specifications. He was accordingly authorized to secure volunteers from trained combat troops that have not been battle-tested. (Mortimer 2013, p. 9)

The 5307th Composite Unit (Provisional) attended training camp for nine weeks until they left for Burma at the end of January 1944. The camp was located on the Betwa River, near the small village of Deogarh in the Central Provinces, India, about 20 miles south of Lallitpur, the Chindits' training camp. This isolated and desolate area had been picked by Wingate, under whose command the Marauders were initially supposed to fight in Burma. The training there was typical for Wingate's indoctrination; namely, forced marches and extensive practice with all of the infantry weapons that would be carried into Burma.

Originally, Galahad was under Mountbatten's operational control and Wingate's training command at Deogarh. Galahad was to furnish three LRP groups to operate under Wingate and enter Burma in 1944 during the dry season; however, Stilwell pestered Mountbatten for American ground forces and ultimately Mountbatten transferred the operational command of the 5307th to Stilwell's Northern Combat Area Command (NCAC) under the direct control of Brigadier-General Frank D. Merrill. They soon received the moniker "Merrill's Marauders" from American war correspondents. Like their Chindit counterparts, they had no heavy artillery or tanks, but

Kachin irregulars, who often comprised merely teenage boys, set up an ambush on a remote jungle trail in Burma. This group is armed (from left to right) with an American M1 Garand rifle, a British Bren light machine gun, and a British Short Magazine Lee-Enfield (SMLE) rifle. (NARA 111-SC-37121-FO)

they were effectively organized for Stilwell's particular "spearheading" role, with special sections for pioneer, demolition, intelligence, and reconnaissance work. Their weapons included M1 carbines, submachine guns, light and heavy machine guns, mortars, and rocket launchers. These weapons and their ammunition meant that each combat team needed a large number of mules, like their Chindit comrades. Merrill used his knowledge of Japanese to gain maximum benefit from the Nisei, the Japanese-speaking Americans, who were used for all aspects of intelligence work.

In April 1942 William Donovan, Roosevelt's appointee as Coordinator of Information (COI), a forerunner of the Office of Strategic Services (OSS), prepared the necessary ground work in Burma for activation of Detachment 101. This was the brainchild of Lieutenant-Colonel Preston Goodfellow, a US Army G-2 liaison attached to the COI; its role was to work behind enemy lines gathering intelligence, ambushing Japanese columns through guerrilla actions, identifying bombing targets for the USAAF, and rescuing downed Allied airmen. Detachment 101 (which never contained more than a few hundred Americans) relied for its manpower on various Burmese tribal groups and, in particular, on the anti-Japanese Kachins. "This early activation date made Detachment 101 one of the earliest American special operations units formed in WWII, predating the First Ranger Battalion, the First Special Service Brigade" (Sacquety 2013, p. 16) as well as Galahad. These tribesmen were virulently anti-Japanese, which stemmed from their loyalty to Westerners from their prewar relationship with Christian missionaries and doctors who cared for them.

In February 1942 Stilwell approved Goodfellow's choice of Captain Carl Eifler, a former US Treasury agent who had also previously served as a lieutenant in a reserve unit Stilwell once commanded, to form Detachment 101. Eifler's charge from Stilwell in northern Burma was to deny the use of the Myitkyina airfield to Japanese fighters. Also, he was to organize Kachin tribesmen to conduct sabotage of railroads, bridges, and river tankers, as well as set up ambushes against Japanese troop detachments, in between Myitkyina and Fort Hertz to the north. Much of what Detachment 101 did was novel and learned via trial and error.

American OSS officers infiltrated Burma in January 1943 to report intelligence, carry out sabotage, and guide Allied bombers to Japanese targets. Later, bases were established into which L-5 Sentinel liaison planes could bring personnel and from which they could evacuate the wounded. It was from these bases that the OSS officers recruited the Kachins of northern Burma. In December 1943, Stilwell issued a directive that Detachment 101 should be augmented to 3,000 Kachins. The Kachin Rangers possessed great jungle skills, and quickly learned how to use radios for effective communication to coordinate their myriad activities. At Fort Hertz in the north, British officers had commanded a battalion of mountain tribesmen called the Northern Kachin Levies. During

Kachin Rangers defend their dug-in positions in Burma while covering a trail. The scout in the center carries an SMLE rifle, while the one at lower right holds an American M3 "grease gun." (USAMHI)

Stilwell's offensive across the Kumon Range in the spring of 1944, Detachment 101 with its 600 Kachin Rangers scouted ahead of Merrill's Marauders and provided flank protection while also attacking Japanese lines of communication.

By the time of its deactivation in July 1945, Detachment 101 had killed 5,428 Japanese and rescued 574 Allied airmen and personnel for a total of approximately 30 Americans and 338 Kachins killed. An additional 10,000 Japanese soldiers were wounded by this group's activities and 78 were taken prisoner. Morevoer, in addition to severing Japanese lines of communication, the importance of Detachment 101's efforts in screening the advances for the three principal Allied offensive forces in northern Burma – Chinese, Chindit, and Marauder – cannot be overemphasized.

On March 5, 1944, Major-General Orde Wingate used his Special Force (3rd Indian Division) to launch his second Chindit invasion of northern Burma, Operation Thursday; however, this one had a major aerial dimension utilizing the Allied 1st Air Commando Group. The functions of the latter force, headed by USAAF colonels Philip Cochran and John Alison, were to provide airlanding of forces, aerial resupply and "artillery," evacuation of wounded, and reinforcement and ordnance buildup at Wingate's new "strongholds" (defensive bases from which the Chindits would launch their disruptive forays principally against the road and railway from Indaw to Myitkyina).

After Wingate's death in a fiery air crash in India on March 24, 1944, the Chindits, although now led by Major-General Walter "Joe" Lentaigne, came under the operational control of Stilwell. One Chindit brigade in particular, Calvert's 77th, would play a major role in Stilwell's assault on Myitkyina. Calvert's battle-weary columns would be given the task in early June 1944 to attack and capture the Japanese-garrisoned town at Mogaung in order to protect Stilwell's left flank on the Myitkyina airfield during the 73-day siege of Myitkyina town. On May 29, 1944, Calvert signaled his desire to Lentaigne to remain in his position in the Gangaw Range and resume guerrilla or LRP methods to harass the Japanese. Calvert summed up his reluctance to become conventional infantry for Stilwell: "Therefore suggest we do not repeat not make flat-out attack against Mogaung in which we risk everything. Can this be given earnest consideration? Only way we can be defeated is by hammering our heads against a brick wall." Lentaigne responded: "You will take Mogaung with 77th Indian Infantry Brigade, less 81 and 82 Columns and levies. Plan at your discretion. Ensure adequate ammunition. Give timings" (quoted in Bidwell 1979, p. 263). Calvert's 77th Indian Infantry Brigade began its attack on Mogaung on June 2, 1944 with a strength of 2,000 men, regrouped into three battalions; the Lancashire Fusiliers and the South Staffords along with the 3/6th Gurkhas, out of the original 3,000 Chindits. To the relief of Calvert, Stilwell's Chinese troops arrived on June 18 with artillery.

An OSS detachment displays captured Japanese *Hinomaru* flags. Evolving slowly from a few OSS officers and non-commissioned officers conducting small-scale sabotage missions, these behind-the-lines Americans and their Kachin Ranger allies became an effective guerrilla force, diverting and killing many Japanese troops, especially north of Myitkyina. (USAMHI)

ORDERS OF BATTLE

Japanese forces

From April 1944, the 18th Division (a triangular one after the Singapore conquest) was part of Thirty-third Army in northern Burma, under the command of Lieutenant-General Honda Masaki. Tanaka's 18th Division comprised three regiments (each Japanese infantry regiment was roughly 2,600 men), each of three battalions. The Japanese division varied greatly in strength, between 12,000 and 22,000 men. The authorized war strength was 19,350 men but operational strength was around 14,200 troops. At the time of the Malaya and Singapore invasion, the total strength of the 18th Division was 22,206 men. Its three infantry regiments were often controlled by an infantry brigade group commanded by a major-general. The Japanese in Burma did not use brigades, except in the case of independent formations like 24th, 72d, and 105th Independent Mixed brigades. The Japanese regiment was the equivalent of a British brigade. At the start of Stilwell's offensive, the 18th Division was well below its full complement due to casualties and illness. It is estimated that at the start of the offensive, Tanaka had a local strength of between 6,300 and 7,000 men in the Hukawng Valley, comprising about five battalions and attached troops (local strength being the estimated strength of units actually present in a given area at any one time and accounting for those evacuated, killed, or missing, and replacements). The structure of the 18th Division at operational strength before casualties was as follows (Madej 1981, pp. 6–14, 47–48):

18TH DIVISION

18TH DIVISION HQ

(Lt. Gen. Tanaka Shinichi; colonel as chief of staff; 350 men)
Administrative Staff
Quartermaster
Medical
Veterinary
Judicial

GENERAL STAFF

(Chief of Staff: Lt. Col. Okoshi Kenji; 75 men)
G1 (Operations and Logistics, Lt. Col.)
G2 (Intelligence, Lt. Col.)
G3 (Supply, Lt. Col.)

DETACHMENTS

18th Signals (Lt. Col. Yamazaki Itsuo; 240 men)
Veterinary (120 men)
Ordnance Duty unit (110 men)
Medical detachment unit (1,110 men)
Field Hospital units (750 men)
Decontamination unit (224 men)
Water purifying unit (250 men)

INFANTRY BRIGADE GROUP

(commanded by a major-general)
HQ (90 men)

55th Infantry Regiment

(Col. Yamazaki Shiro; 2,850 men in each regiment)
HQ (98 men)
Signals Company (133 men)
Artillery (123 men)
Antitank (72 men)
3 battalions (c.1,000 men each, commanded by a major)
Battalion HQ (103 men)
Four Rifle companies (180 men each, in three platoons of four sections each)
Machine Gun Company (120 men)
Battalion artillery platoon (44 men)

56th Infantry Regiment

(Col. Nagahisa) – see 55th Infantry Regiment organization

114th Infantry Regiment

(Col. Fusayasu Maruyama) – see 55th Infantry Regiment organization

18th Mountain Artillery Regiment

(Col. Hidohira Takao, 3,500 men)
HQ
Three Battalions (980 men)

12th Engineer Regiment

(Lt. Col. Miyama Tadao, 956 men)
Three companies (250 men)
Material platoon (50 men)

12th Transport Regiment

  (Lt. Col. Mizutani Torakichi, 1,810 men)

  Four Draught companies (350 men)

  Two Motor companies (205 men)

13th Rapid Response (Reconnaissance) Battalion

12th Construction (Bridging) Regiment

DIVISIONAL ARMAMENT

The total armament of the division at full strength was:

Rifles	9,000
Light machine guns	273
Grenade dischargers	264
Heavy machine guns	78
20mm antitank guns	18
37mm antitank guns	14
47mm antitank guns	8
70mm battalion guns	18
75mm regimental guns	12
75mm mountain guns	36

Allied forces

NORTHERN COMBAT AREA COMMAND

(Lt. Gen. Joseph W. Stilwell)

CHINESE ARMY IN INDIA

Chinese 38th Division (Lt. Gen. Sun Li-jen)

  (equivalent in strength to a British brigade)

    Divisional Artillery Headquarters

    Two Artillery battalions

    Engineer Battalion

    Signals Battalion

    Transportation Battalion

    Reconnaissance Company

    Gas, Medical, Veterinary, Field Hospital, and Special Service platoons

  112th Infantry Regiment

  (equivalent in strength to a British battalion)

    Headquarters Detachment

    Mortar Company

    Antitank Company

    Transport Company (pack animal)

    Transport Company (motor)

    Signals Platoon

    Special Service Platoon

    Medical/Veterinary Detachment

    Three infantry battalions, each containing:

      Three rifle companies

      Machine-gun Company

      Headquarters Detachment

  113th Infantry Regiment

    See 112th Infantry Regiment organization

  114th Infantry Regiment

    See 112th Infantry Regiment organization

Chinese 22d Division (Lt. Gen. Liao Yao-hsiang)

  Divisional Artillery Headquarters

  Two Artillery battalions

  Engineer Battalion

  Signals Battalion

  Transportation Battalion

  Reconnaissance Company

  Gas, Medical, Veterinary, Field Hospital, and Special Service platoons

  64th Infantry Regiment

    See 112th Infantry Regiment organization, 38th Division

  65th Infantry Regiment

    See 112th Infantry Regiment organization, 38th Division

  66th Infantry Regiment

    See 112th Infantry Regiment organization, 38th Division

1st Provisional Tank Group (Col. Rothwell H. Brown)

This unit was the only Chinese Army formation, under Stilwell, commanded by an American and a Chinese vice-commander, Colonel Chao Chen-yu, with an American medium tank platoon in support. The number of Americans increased steadily from the initial component of 11 officers and 9 enlisted men to a peak strength of 29 officers and 222 enlisted men. All of its equipment was American including M3 light (Stuart) and M4 medium (Sherman) tanks.

5307th Composite Unit (Provisional) (Brig. Gen. Frank D. Merrill)

  (deputy commander Col. Charles Hunter)

  1st Battalion (Lt. Col. William L. Osborne)

  (35 officers, 928 enlisted men; 139 horses and mules)

    Red Combat Team

      Headquarters Platoon

      Intelligence and Reconnaissance (I&R) Platoon

      Pioneer and Demolition Platoon

      Medical detachment

      Heavy Weapons Platoon (three heavy machine guns, four 81mm mortars)

      Rifle companies (one and a half in one battalion's Combat teams, two in the other)

      Half of Company Headquarters in one battalion Combat Team only

    White Combat Team

      (see Red Combat Team, 1st Battalion organization)

  2d Battalion (Lt. Col. George A. McGee, Jr.)

    Blue Combat Team

      (see Red Combat Team, 1st Battalion organization)

    Green Combat Team

      (see Red Combat Team, 1st Battalion organization)

  3d Battalion (Lt. Col. Charles E. Beach)

    Orange Combat Team

      (see Red Combat Team, 1st Battalion organization)

    Khaki Combat Team

      (see Red Combat Team, 1st Battalion organization)

  Armament of a battalion:

    181 M1 carbines

    7 heavy machine guns

    6 light machine guns

    102 submachine guns

    10 60mm mortars

7 81mm mortars

4 pistols (flare)

54 Browning Automatic Rifles

624 M1 Garand rifles

6 rockets

Ledo Road Construction Troops (Brig. Gen. Lewis Pick)

US Army 849th Engineer Aviation Battalion

US Army 1883d Engineer Aviation Battalion

US Army 382d Engineer Battalion (Separate)

US Army 45th Quartermaster Regiment

US Army 209th Combat Engineer Battalion

US Army 1905th Engineer Aviation Battalion

SPECIAL FORCE (3RD INDIAN DIVISION)

(Maj. Gen. Orde C. Wingate)

The brigades were subdivided into single battalions from various regiments for listing in the order of battle as such; however, each battalion was further divided into two columns.

77th Indian Infantry Brigade (Brig. James Michael Calvert), 25 Column HQ

Mixed Field Company, RE/IE

1st King's Regiment (Liverpool), 81 and 82 columns

1st Lancashire Fusiliers, 20 and 50 columns

1st South Staffordshire Regiment, 38 and 80 columns

3/6th Gurkha Rifles, 36 and 63 columns

Medical and Veterinary detachments

111th Indian Infantry Brigade (Maj. Gen. Walter "Joe" Lentaigne from March 27, 1944), 48 Column HQ

Mixed Field Company, RE/IE

2nd King's Own Royal Regiment, 41 and 46 columns

1st Cameronians, 26 and 90 columns

3/4th Gurkha Rifles, 30 and 40 columns

4/9th Gurkha Rifles, 49 and 94 columns

Medical and Veterinary detachments

14th British Infantry Brigade (Brig. Thomas Brodie), 59 Column HQ

54th Field Company, RE

1st Bedfordshire and Hertfordshire Regiment, 16 and 61 columns

7th Leicestershire Regiment, 47 and 74 columns

2nd Black Watch, 42 and 73 columns

2nd York and Lancaster Regiment, 65 and 84 columns

Medical detachment

16th British Infantry Brigade (Brig. Bernard E. Fergusson), 99 Column HQ

2nd Field Company, RE

51st/69th Field Regiment, RA (employed as LRP infantry), 51 and 69 columns

2nd Queen's Royal Regiment (West Surrey), 21 and 22 columns

2nd Leicestershire Regiment, 17 and 71 columns

45th Reconnaissance Regiment, 45 and 54 columns

Medical detachment

23rd British Infantry Brigade (Brig. Lance E. C. M. Perowne), 32 Column HQ

12th Field Company, RE

60th Field Regiment, RA (employed as LRP infantry), 60 and 68 columns

2nd Duke of Wellington's Regiment, 33 and 76 columns

4th Border Regiment, 34 and 55 columns

1st Essex Regiment, 44 and 56 columns

Medical detachment

3rd West African Brigade (Brig. Argyle H. Gillmore, later by Brig. Abdy H. G. Ricketts), 10 Column HQ

7th West African Field Company

6th Nigeria Regiment, 39 and 66 columns

7th Nigeria Regiment, 29 and 35 columns

12th Nigeria Regiment, 12 and 43 columns

3rd West African Field Ambulance

Divisional troops

219th Field Park Company, RE

Detachment 2nd Burma Rifles

145th Brigade Company, RASC

61st Air Supply Company, RASC

2nd Indian Air Supply Company, RASC

Attached troops

Four troops 160th Field Regiment, RA

Four troops 69th Light Anti-Aircraft Regiment, RA

3/9th Gurkha Rifles

Composition of each column:

(306 men for a British column; 369 for a Gurkha one)

HQ section (8 men)

Infantry company

(5 British officers; company commander (captain), 3 platoon leaders (lieutenants), and 1 company sergeant major, 110 other ranks)

Three platoons (each 36 men) each with 3 rifle sections (each with 7 riflemen, a 2-man Bren team, a 2-man Boyes AT rifle team, and a sergeant as section leader; NCOs had Thompson or Sten submachine guns)

RAF section (5 men)

Signals squad (5 men)

Medical section (5 men)

Sabotage or sapper group (platoon strength, 29 men)

Regimental signalers section (6 men)

Burma Rifle platoon to provide scouts (45 men)

Support platoon (31 men) with 2 3in. mortars and 2 Vickers machine guns

Second line transport platoon (57 men) with mules

1ST AIR COMMANDO GROUP, USAAF

(Col. Philip G. Cochran and Col. John R. Alison)

288 aircraft manned with 600 of all ranks to provide crews and servicing (a ratio of 1:2, whereas normally it would be 1:5 or 1:10)

100 Waco CG-4A gliders

100 light planes, mainly L-5 Sentinels with a few L-1 Vigilants

30 P-51A Mustang fighter/ground attack aircraft

20 B-25H Mitchell medium bombers

20 C-47 Dakota transports

12 UC-64 Norseman transports

6 Sikorsky prototype helicopters

OPPOSING PLANS

JAPANESE PLANS

At first, the Japanese believed that northern Burma was unsuitable as a base for conducting offensive operations. In September 1942, Lieutenant-General Mutaguchi Renya (then 18th Division commander) told the commander of Fifteenth Army, Lieutenant-General Iida Shojiro, that the terrain in northern Burma, with its endless jungles and mountains, was so formidable that his division would be unable to cross the mountains into Assam or be supported there. This stymied a Fifteenth Army preliminary plan to advance through the Hukawng Valley and on to Assam's air depots in a bid to sever Chiang Kai-shek's air supply route, the "Hump." By early 1943, two IJA divisions, the 18th and 33d (then commanded by Lieutenant-General Sakurai Shozo), were deployed facing to the north and west in order to hold northern Burma and the Chindwin River with a skeleton force of only one or two battalions, while the other battalions refitted and recuperated from their conquest of Burma.

In the winter of 1943, during Operation Longcloth, Wingate would teach Mutaguchi that a large force could successfully cross the hills and Chindwin River separating India and Burma. Mutaguchi's 18th Division garrisoned the area through which Wingate's Chindit columns would operate during Longcloth. The Japanese leadership in Burma was initially content simply to garrison the country. The Japanese 18th Division had three regiments initially divided for both patrolling and garrisoning. Two regiments (the 55th and 56th) would be dedicated to the Hukawng Valley, while the third regiment (the 114th) was stationed at division headquarters at Myitkyina. With the passage of time and not merely waiting for an Allied attack, the 18th Division's battalions abandoned garrisoning and began vigorous patrolling, established outposts in the Hukawng Valley, and acted against the activities of British-led Kachin insurgents from Fort Hertz, the last British bastion in northern Burma, at Sumprabum north of Myitkyina.

On March 27, 1943 Mutaguchi was promoted to lead Fifteenth Army in northern Burma; his successor at 18th Division was Tanaka Shinichi. Mutaguchi had scrutinized Wingate's tactics and his use of the Burmese terrain, and concluded, as the Chindits had demonstrated during Operation Longcloth in early 1943, that troops would be mobile with pack transport only in northern and western Burma during the dry season. The Chindits had shown that it was possible for units to attack across the main north–south grain of the rivers and mountains of Burma. The Japanese general's revelation, along with intelligence of the British buildup at Imphal, convinced Mutaguchi that he must eventually attack Imphal and Kohima to preempt another large-scale British invasion of Burma from India in 1944. However, prior to that invasion, Mutaguchi argued that Fifteenth Army's line of defense should be moved westwards, to at least the Chindwin River, or even possibly to the hills on the Assam–Burma border.

On April 11, 1943 Mutaguchi was relieved of the responsibility of looking after northern Burma and was given the single task of planning the Imphal/Kohima offensive, Operation *U-Go*. The best course would be to attack the British before they had time to complete their preparations for an offensive and capture their base at Imphal, thereby preventing them from launching an offensive into Burma. The end of summer 1943 found the IJA planning an offensive for the dry season of early 1944.

As for the Japanese plans in northern Burma during December 1943, Tanaka had no intention of 18th Division remaining solely on the defensive. The Japanese referred to the Hukawng Valley as the "Valley of Death," not out of fear of the enemy but rather the harsh terrain and pestilence that characterized that setting. Nonetheless, Tanaka planned to attack with his 55th and 56th regiments, leaving the 114th Infantry Regiment to garrison Myitkyina. However, Mutaguchi overruled him, since the Fifteenth Army commander was actively planning for his attack on Imphal set for March 1944. Tanaka was told that any movement of reinforcements with 18th Division troops north of the Tanai must have Mutaguchi's approval since the latter could not spare any additional transport to provide logistical support to the 18th Division. Tanaka was told that at the very least he could counterattack in the area around Maingkwan, near the south end of the Hukawng Valley, but it was imperative that he hold Kamaing, which was just south of the Jambu Bum, the ridgeline that separated the Hukawng from the Mogaung Valley. Tanaka's plans now incorporated the weather, since he was hoping that when the monsoon rains in May and June began, the Allied

Major-General Joseph Stilwell leads the "Walkout" from Burma. After learning that the Japanese had outstripped his withdrawal towards Myitkyina, Stilwell and a party of 114 British, American, and Burmese began their trek both overland and by waterways. They crossed the Chindwin River in dugouts and ferries at Homalin, hours before a Japanese cavalry detachment arrived there. Setting a demanding pace, Stilwell managed to extricate his entire party to India. (USAMHI)

Operations *U-Go* and Thursday, March–June 1944

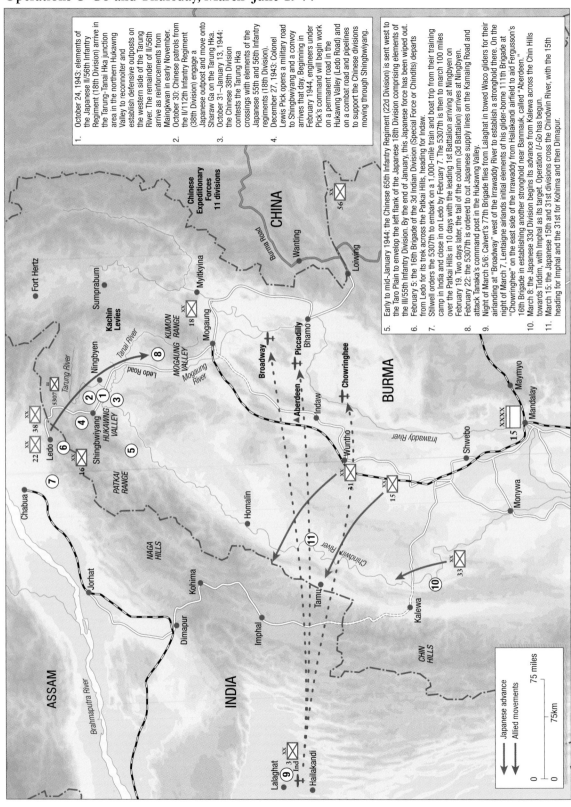

1. October 24, 1943: elements of the Japanese II/56th Infantry Regiment (18th Division) arrive in the Tarung-Tanai Hka junction area in the northern Hukawng Valley to reconnoiter and establish defensive outposts on the western side of the Tarung River. The remainder of II/56th arrive as reinforcements from Maingkwan in early November. October 30: Chinese patrols from the II/112th Infantry Regiment (38th Division) engage a Japanese outpost and move onto Sharaw Ga on the Tarung Hka.

2. October 31–January 13, 1944: the Chinese 38th Division contests the Tarung Hka crossings with elements of the Japanese 55th and 56th Infantry regiments (18th Division).

3. December 27, 1943: Colonel Lewis Pick opens a military road to Shingbwiyang and a convoy arrives that day. Beginning in February 1944, engineers under Pick's command will begin work on a permanent road in the Hukawng Valley (Ledo Road) and on a combat road and pipelines to support the Chinese divisions moving through Shingbwiyang.

4. Early to mid-January 1944: the Chinese 65th Infantry Regiment (22d Division) is sent west to the Taro Plain to envelop the left flank of the Japanese 18th Division comprising elements of the III/55th Infantry Division. By the end of January, this Japanese force has been wiped out.

5. February 5: the 16th Brigade of the 3d Indian Division (Special Force or Chindits) departs from Ledo for its trek across the Patkai Hills, heading for Indaw.

6. Stilwell orders the 5307th to embark on a 1,000-mile train and boat trip from their training camp in India and close in on Ledo by February 7. The 5307th is then to march 100 miles over the Patkai Hills in 10 days with the leading 1st Battalion arriving at Ningbyen on February 19. Two days later, the tail of the column (3d Battalion) arrives at Ningbyen.

7. February 22: the 5307th is ordered to cut Japanese supply lines on the Kamaing Road and attack Tanaka's command post in the Hukawng Valley.

8. Night of March 5/6: Calvert's 77th Brigade flies from Lalaghat in towed Waco gliders for their airlanding at "Broadway" west of the Irrawaddy River to establish a stronghold there. On the night of March 7, Lentaigne airlands initial elements of his glider-borne 111th Brigade at "Chowringhee" on the east side of the Irrawaddy from Hailakandi airfield to aid Fergusson's 16th Brigade in establishing another stronghold near Banmauk, called "Aberdeen."

9. March 8: the Japanese 33d Division begins its advance from Kalewa across the Chin Hills towards Tiddim, with Imphal as its target. Operation *U-Go* has begun.

10. March 15: the Japanese 15th and 31st divisions cross the Chindwin River, with the 15th heading for Imphal and the 31st for Kohima and then Dimapur.

Chinese Expeditionary Forces 11 divisions

CHINA

Burma Road

Wanting

Loiwing

56

Fort Hertz

Sumprabum

Kachin Levies

Myitkyina

Mogaung

KUMON RANGE

18

Ningbyen

Tanai River

Ledo Road

MOGAUNG VALLEY

Mogaung River

Tarung River

5307

38

22

Ledo

Shingbwiyang

HUKAWNG VALLEY

16

PATKAI RANGE

Chabua

Jorhat

Kohima

Dimapur

Homalin

NAGA HILLS

ASSAM

INDIA

Imphal

Tamu

Chindwin River

Kalewa

CHIN HILLS

33

Lalaghat

Hailakandi

3 Ind

Broadway

Aberdeen

Piccadilly

Bhamo

Indaw

Chowringhee

Wuntho

31

15

Irrawaddy River

Shwebo

Monywa

BURMA

Maymyo

Mandalay

15

Japanese advance

Allied movements

0   75 miles
0   75km

advance would stall. Thus, Tanaka's delaying action down the Hukawng Valley held some advantages for his men, such as familiarity with the terrain and the support of his divisional field mountain artillery regiment possessing 12 75mm mountain guns and four 150mm howitzers. The Japanese strength in the Hukawng Valley was roughly 6,300 men. Myitkyina was to be strongly held to block any attack from China.

ALLIED PLANS

After the "Walkout" from Burma to Assam, Stilwell was preoccupied with a future capture of Myitkyina. At a personal level, for the US Army's recognized expert on China and its culture, it was a matter of restoring pride or "face" by conducting an offensive in northern Burma, with the prize being Myitkyina's seizure. His impromptu remarks at an Indian press conference in April 1942 resonated his commitment as he plainly stated: "I claim we got a hell of a beating. We got run out of Burma and it is humiliating as hell. I think we ought to find out what caused it, go back and retake it" (Stilwell 1991, p. 106). To this end, since the autumn of 1942 US Army engineers, led by Brigadier-General Lewis Pick, had been constructing the Ledo Road with the intent to cross a reconquered northern Burma and ultimately link with the Burma Road at Mong Yu, which lies between Bhamo and Lashio, south of Myitkyina.

The official US Army history of the campaign in Burma indicates:
The terrain feature on which the campaign, seen in its largest sense, currently focused was the town of Myitkyina … Lying in the center of north Burma, at the southern tip of the mountain range or Hump over which the transports flew to China, Myitkyina had strategic advantages to which the Joint and Combined Chiefs attached great importance. Were Myitkyina and its airfields in Allied hands, the transports of the ATC could fly a lower, broader route to China. Were Myitkyina in Allied hands, the Ledo Road and its companion pipelines could link with the prewar communications net of northern Burma, [thereby] Myitkyina would become a great supply center, and the end of China's blockade would be at hand. To get to Myitkyina, Stilwell would have to move south down the long corridor of the Hukawng Valley and across the Jambu Bum ridge into the Mogaung Valley … The southern exit from the Mogaung valley is within easy march of Myitkyina, and the Irrawaddy Valley that forms so much of central Burma … The principal barrier between Stilwell and Myitkyina was the three regiments of the Japanese 18th Division. These skilled veterans under the competent leadership of General Tanaka could be counted on to make good use of the several dominant terrain features that lay between Stilwell's troops and the streets, houses, bazaars, and temples of Myitkyina. (Romanus and Sunderland 1970, p. 121)

A Chinese infantryman at Stilwell's training facility for his CAI at Ramgarh, which would become the major striking portion of his Northern Combat Area Command. Initially, the remnants of the Chinese 38th and 22d divisions, which fought in Burma in 1942, were brought to Ramgarh for reinforcement, refitting, rearming, and training. Since Stilwell agreed to serve under Slim, he set up NCAC to keep the Chinese divisions and Merrill's Marauders under his control. (USAMHI)

In order to keep China in the war as well as expand the width of the air-supply corridor from India to Yunnan Province ("the Hump"), the eventuality of building a new road and pipeline from Ledo in India to ultimately join the Burma Road south of Myitkyina was apparent to the Allied high command at the "Quadrant" and "Sextant" Conferences in August in Quebec and November 1943 in Cairo, respectively. The Combined Chiefs of Staff (CCS) ordered Stilwell to train Chiang Kai-shek's 38th and 22d divisions in Ramgarh, India and, along with the 5307th Composite Unit (Provisional), to capture the railway and airfield hub at Myitkyina and the town of Mogaung. Both towns were in the Irrawaddy Valley, the most hospitable part of northern Burma, and on the rail and road network of prewar Burma, so when the Ledo Road reached them the engineering problem would be one of improving existing facilities rather than constructing new ones in the virgin wilderness. Thus, the capture of the Mogaung–Myitkyina area was the vital requirement for completing the Ledo Road and opening a ground line of communications, with an all-weather road and a gasoline pipeline, to China.

Although the outcomes of the Chindits' Operation Longcloth in February 1943 have remained controversial, the ability of properly trained British and Gurkha soldiers to fight and survive in jungle combat nullified the prevailing dogma of the IJA infantryman's superiority there. Thus, coincident with Stilwell's mission and with CCS support at both the "Quadrant" and "Sextant" conferences, Wingate planned a second, even larger Burma invasion with six brigades (Operation Thursday) for March 1944. Wingate would utilize glider-borne and C-47 transport airlanding of infantry; "stronghold" defensive areas to amplify Japanese lines of communication interdiction; and the 1st Air Commando Group's aerial attack and resupply capabilities. In early January 1944, Stilwell, looking to the future, asked Wingate to move the American LRP group (Galahad), which Wingate had trained in India, to the Hukawng Valley. Wingate agreed, but privately he was

The Allied leaders met in Cairo in November and December 1943 at the "Sextant" Conference. Shown here are Generalissimo Chiang Kai-shek (seated far left), President Franklin Roosevelt (seated center), and Prime Minister Winston Churchill (seated right). Major-General Stilwell stands behind Roosevelt, while Admiral Lord Louis Mountbatten, leader of SEAC, stands to the far right. "Sextant" cancelled the amphibious operation that Chiang Kai-shek wanted to reopen the Burma Road. Instead, Roosevelt moved forward to give full support to Stilwell's plans in northern Burma to advance through the Hukawng and Mogaung valleys, drive out Tanaka's 18th Division, build the Ledo Road and gasoline/water pipelines and reopen the Burma Road. Churchill expressed grave reluctance at fighting a land campaign in northern Burma. (USAMHI)

disappointed to lose this formation. Wingate's orders for Operation Thursday were issued by Slim and Lieutenant-General George E. Stratemeyer, commander Far East Air Forces (FEAF), on February 4, 1944. The Chindit leader was instructed to help the advance of Stilwell's force from Ledo, among other tasks such as creating a favorable situation for the Chinese to advance from the Yunnan across the Salween River and to inflict maximum confusion, damage, and loss on the enemy forces in northern Burma.

In a memorandum to the British prime minister dated February 25, 1944, President Roosevelt made clear his strategic vision:

> I have always advocated the development of China as a base for the support of our Pacific advances, and now that the war has taken a greater turn in our favor … it is mandatory therefore that we make every effort to increase the flow of supplies into China. This can only be done by increasing the air tonnage or by opening a road through Burma. Our occupation of Myitkyina will enable us immediately to increase the air-lift to China by providing an intermediate air-transport base as well as by increasing the protection of the air route. General Stilwell is confident that his Chinese–American Force can seize Myitkyina by the end of this dry season. (Churchill 1951, p. 562)

However, the British high command had a sharply different strategic view, which was to continually fuel Stilwell's vociferous, acerbic Anglophobic proclivity. Churchill later wrote:

> I had always advocated air aid to China and the improvement of the air route and protection of the airfields … however, [the Americans] pressed as a matter of the highest urgency and importance the making of a motor road from their great air starting-point at Ledo through five hundred miles of jungles and mountains into China … I disliked intensely the prospect of a large-scale campaign in northern Burma. One could not choose a worse place for fighting the Japanese … We of course wanted to recapture Burma, but we did not want to have to do it by land advances from slender communications and across the most forbidding fighting country imaginable. The south of Burma, with its port of Rangoon, was far more valuable than the north. (Churchill 1951, pp. 560–61)

The ever-pragmatic US Army Chief of Staff, General George C. Marshall, although supportive of his protégée, also realized the potential pitfalls of Stilwell's mission to conquer northern Burma and capture Myitkyina:

> The mission … given General Stilwell in Asia was one of the most difficult of the war. He was out at the end of the thinnest supply line of all; the demands of the war in Europe and the Pacific campaign, which were clearly the most vital to final victory, exceeded our resources … General Stilwell could have only what was left and that was extremely thin … He faced an extremely difficult political problem and his purely military problem of opposing large numbers of enemy with few resources was unmatched in any theatre. (Quoted in Eldridge 1946, p. 160)

Also, as noted by the official American historians of the CBI theater, "one of the noteworthy aspects of the North Burma Campaign of 1943–44 is that the logistical preparations, the planning, and the fighting proceeded simultaneously" (Romanus and Sunderland 1970, p. 48).

THE CAMPAIGN

DOWN THE HUKAWNG VALLEY

Chinese troops and engineers construct an improvised pontoon bridge over a Burmese *chaung* (small stream). River dugouts lashed together by wire serve as suspension while wooden slats form the bridge's single-file deck. (USAMHI)

Stilwell's northern Burma campaign was set to begin on December 1, 1943, after the earlier cancellation in February 1943, leaving time for SEAC to settle on a plan to coordinate this advance with the British one in the Arakan coastal region in southern Burma. There were a number of geographical areas that would have to be seized by Stilwell in order to reconquer northern Burma. First was the Hukawng Valley, into which drains a whole system of rivers – all tributaries of the larger Tanai Hka, which flows northwest in a series of loops until it meets the wall of the Patkai Hills, in the north, where it changes its name to the Chindwin River and turns south. The Tarung Hka, flowing southwest, enters the Tanai Hka, which during the dry season is about 200yd wide but becomes much wider with the monsoons. The point at which the Tarung enters the Tanai Hka is about six miles to the southwest of the village of Yupbang Ga. Both the Tarung and Tanai were in the direct path of the US engineers, under Pick, building the Ledo Road. The Tanai Hka area had to be cleared of the enemy to give the road engineers safe access to the Shingbwiyang clearing in the northern Hukawng Valley.

Both the Allies and the Japanese wanted control of the fords across these waterways to serve as springboards for their respective offensives. Stilwell wanted to move down the Hukawng Valley, with the Ledo Road construction proceeding behind him, into the Mogaung Valley and on to Myitkyina before the spring monsoon season erupted. According to Stilwell, his campaign in northern Burma was "to go in through a rat hole and dig the hole as we go" (quoted in Tuchman 1970, p. 416). According to Tuchman:

The rat hole has a series of three valleys: the Hukawng, terminating in a ridge called the Jambu Bum; next the Mogaung valley leading to the main north–south railroad; and on the other side of the railroad the broad Irrawaddy Valley, Burma's central corridor. Myitkyina, the northernmost major Japanese garrison and air base, lay on the railroad and river 40 miles below Mogaung; from here a road descended southward to connect with the old Burma Road into China. The slot assigned to the NCAC, thick with jungle growth and threaded by overgrown trails which allowed progress of sometimes as little as a mile an hour, and edged by mountain ranges carved by directionless ridges by the run offs from heavy rains, was as forbidding fighting country as any in the world. (Tuchman 1970, p. 416)

Tanaka had deployed the 55th and 56th Infantry regiments of his division to the Hukawng Valley, while he kept his third regiment, the 114th, stationed at Myitkyina. After Mutaguchi decided in September 1943 to launch Operation *U-Go* against General Slim in Assam in March 1944, Tanaka knew that he would not receive any reinforcements in the Hukawng Valley. In Tanaka's view, the Hukawng Valley was an awful place to fight. From 15 to 50 miles across east to west, it extended north to south for 130 miles; was transected by many rivers; and was easily turned into a marshy quagmire by the monsoon, creating a nest for cholera and malaria. Tanaka, in early November 1943, was contemplating a mid-December offensive, which was "to move the main strength of the [18th Division] from Ningbyen towards Shingbwiyang and the exit of the mountain road on the India–Burma border to attack and destroy the American and Chinese forces which would advance in a long column through the tortuous Ledo Road in India" (quoted in Romanus and Sunderland 1970, p. 47). At the Tarung Hka's eastern fords, Tanaka had positioned elements of the 55th and 56th Infantry regiments in outposts.

Although Stilwell's North Burma campaign was officially to commence on December 1, 1943, Brigadier-General Haydon Boatner, CAI commander and Stilwell's deputy, ordered Sun Li-jen to move three battalions of the 112th Infantry Regiment (38th Division) on October 5, 1943 along three widely separated tracks, to act as a shield for the advancing Ledo Road construction crews. Liao Yao-hsiang's 22d Division was still training at Ramgarh. The 2/112th was to take up positions at Sharaw Ga and Ningbyen on the Tarung Hka, and the 1/112th was tasked with occupying Yupbang Ga, also on the Tarung in the northern end of the Hukawng Valley. By controlling the fords at these sites along the Tarung, the Chinese would prevent the

Japanese troops often encircled the enemy through the jungle to get behind them and set up a roadblock or ambush. However, this limited the use of pack animals, so IJA infantrymen, shown here emerging from the jungle, would often break down their artillery pieces into smaller component parts and manhandle them on the route. (USAMHI)

Chinese troops attacking across an open area in the vicinity of a Burmese town under artillery cover. The soldier to the rear is carrying a British Bren gun, which was relatively light at 22.5lb (empty). (NARA 111-SC-197903-9).

Japanese from moving further west into the Hukawng Valley. However, on October 24, a reconnaissance company of the 2/56th Infantry Regiment of the IJA 18th Division arrived in the Tarung Hka area unopposed and began to construct defensive fortifications and outposts there on the western bank of the river in the same locations of Sharaw Ga, Ningbyen, and Yupbang Ga that the Chinese 112th Infantry Regiment's battalions were to advance to. Further elements of the Japanese 2/56th Infantry Regiment were at Maingkwan, situated on a road to the southeast; the remaining regimental troops were sent forward to the northern outposts as reinforcements in early November.

On October 30, the Chinese collided with strong elements of the IJA 56th Infantry Regiment led by Colonel Nagahisa, in their outposts on the Tarung Hka at Sharaw Ga, forcing the Japanese back into a nearby village. As the Chinese continued their advance, they began taking heavy casualties from extensive and accurate Japanese gun and mortar fire. Similarly, the Chinese 1/112th encountered the Japanese at Yupbang Ga, but they were well entrenched and capably commanded, resulting in the isolation of the Chinese by typical Japanese infantry tactics: roadblock and encirclement, tempting the Chinese to attack the former. As Japanese strength continued to grow in

An American aircrew pushes out supplies, mostly animal feed, to drop free-fall from a C-47 Dakota transport from relatively low altitude. A considerable amount of feed was necessary to sustain the pack animals. (USAMHI)

numbers along the Tarung, a company of the Chinese 1/112th was completely destroyed on November 2. The 112th's regimental command post was captured by the Japanese on the night of November 3 and the dwindling Chinese survivors had to be supplied by air drop. An abortive attempt to break through to the 1/112th by a company of the 1/114th in mid-November was made; the surrounded Chinese now had to wait for the remainder of the 38th Division to get to the front.

Stilwell, returning from the "Sextant" Conference, arrived at Shingbwiyang on December 21 with his offensive already a month late. He observed first-hand that the Japanese at Yupbang Ga had isolated the Chinese 112th Infantry Regiment and that relief attempts had already failed, and he lambasted his Chinese officers while also arranging a coordinated attack. Confronted with the Japanese holding the river fords at Yupbang Ga and Ningbyen, Stilwell noted that the Tanai Hka ford at Kantau, due west of Yupbang Ga, was not defended by Tanaka's troops, thereby creating a potential exit to the south across the river. With the Japanese 56th Infantry Regiment's battalions positioned parallel to the Tarung, within 30yd of Sun Li-jen's Chinese troops, Stilwell hoped to cross the Tanai at the unguarded Kantau ford and place one of his Chinese regiments in Tanaka's rear, thereby cutting off the Japanese forces north of the Tanai. However, in order to conduct a successful southern envelopment of the Japanese and relieve the 112th, Stilwell would need a strong offensive move against Yupbang Ga, by the Chinese 1/114th under Major Peng Ke-li with the 5th and 6th Artillery batteries. This attack was launched at 1000hrs on December 24 after an artillery barrage, which alerted the Japanese. Despite only some of the Japanese outposts being destroyed by the Chinese, contact was made with the 1/112th at 1515hrs. Tanaka commented after the war: "the unexpected stubbornness of the Chinese troops in the fighting around Yupbang Ga led the Japanese to believe that troops that faced them were far superior in both the quality of their fighting and in the equipment to the Chinese troops they

The Chinese crew of a 105mm howitzer of the 38th Division fires on Japanese positions at Warazup in the Mogaung Valley. Experience had taught Sun Li-jen's troops that mortar rounds and direct machine-gun fire were usually ineffective against fortified pillboxes; high-caliber artillery or direct tank-gun fire were needed to reduce the positions from afar, or grenades, flamethrowers, and explosive satchels from close up. (NARA 111-SC-302220FA)

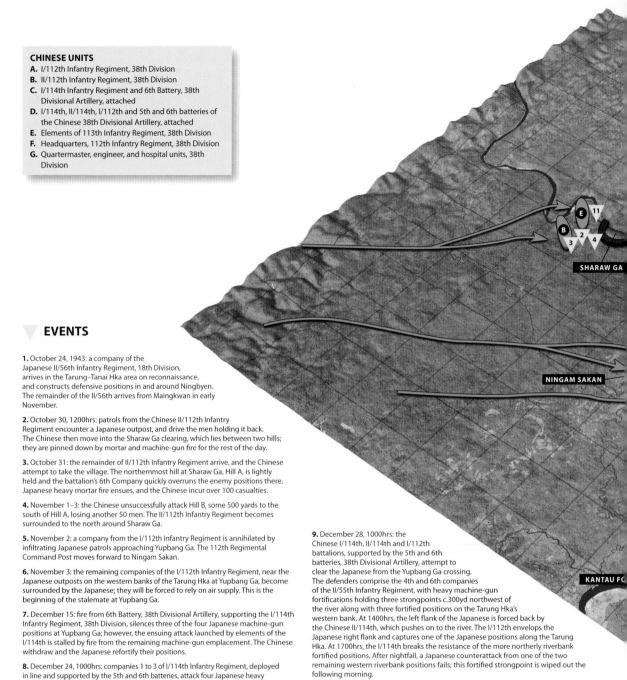

CHINESE UNITS
A. I/112th Infantry Regiment, 38th Division
B. II/112th Infantry Regiment, 38th Division
C. I/114th Infantry Regiment and 6th Battery, 38th Divisional Artillery, attached
D. I/114th, II/114th, I/112th and 5th and 6th batteries of the Chinese 38th Divisional Artillery, attached
E. Elements of 113th Infantry Regiment, 38th Division
F. Headquarters, 112th Infantry Regiment, 38th Division
G. Quartermaster, engineer, and hospital units, 38th Division

SHARAW GA

NINGAM SAKAN

KANTAU FC

EVENTS

1. October 24, 1943: a company of the Japanese II/56th Infantry Regiment, 18th Division, arrives in the Tarung–Tanai Hka area on reconnaissance, and constructs defensive positions in and around Ningbyen. The remainder of the II/56th arrives from Maingkwan in early November.

2. October 30, 1200hrs: patrols from the Chinese II/112th Infantry Regiment encounter a Japanese outpost, and drive the men holding it back. The Chinese then move into the Sharaw Ga clearing, which lies between two hills; they are pinned down by mortar and machine-gun fire for the rest of the day.

3. October 31: the remainder of II/112th Infantry Regiment arrive, and the Chinese attempt to take the village. The northernmost hill at Sharaw Ga, Hill A, is lightly held and the battalion's 6th Company quickly overruns the enemy positions there. Japanese heavy mortar fire ensues, and the Chinese incur over 100 casualties.

4. November 1–3: the Chinese unsuccessfully attack Hill B, some 500 yards to the south of Hill A, losing another 50 men. The II/112th Infantry Regiment becomes surrounded to the north around Sharaw Ga.

5. November 2: a company from the I/112th Infantry Regiment is annihilated by infiltrating Japanese patrols approaching Yupbang Ga. The 112th Regimental Command Post moves forward to Ningam Sakan.

6. November 3: the remaining companies of the I/112th Infantry Regiment, near the Japanese outposts on the western banks of the Tarung Hka at Yupbang Ga, become surrounded by the Japanese; they will be forced to rely on air supply. This is the beginning of the stalemate at Yupbang Ga.

7. December 15: fire from 6th Battery, 38th Divisional Artillery, supporting the I/114th Infantry Regiment, 38th Division, silences three of the four Japanese machine-gun positions at Yupbang Ga; however, the ensuing attack launched by elements of the I/114th is stalled by fire from the remaining machine-gun emplacement. The Chinese withdraw and the Japanese refortify their positions.

8. December 24, 1000hrs: companies 1 to 3 of I/114th Infantry Regiment, deployed in line and supported by the 5th and 6th batteries, attack four Japanese heavy machine-gun emplacements set in square formation, which are blocking the way to the surrounded I/112th survivors. At 1300hrs, under artillery barrage, the three Chinese companies make contact with one another inside the "square," and subsequently with the 1/112th. At 1545hrs, a Japanese counterattack is launched and repulsed. By 0900hrs the following day, the last Japanese pocket of resistance has been wiped out. However, the ford across the Tarung Hka at Yupbang Ga still remains in Japanese hands.

9. December 28, 1000hrs: the Chinese I/114th, II/114th and I/112th battalions, supported by the 5th and 6th batteries, 38th Divisional Artillery, attempt to clear the Japanese from the Yupbang Ga crossing. The defenders comprise the 4th and 6th companies of the II/55th Infantry Regiment, with heavy machine-gun fortifications holding three strongpoints c.300yd northwest of the river along with three fortified positions on the Tarung Hka's western bank. At 1400hrs, the left flank of the Japanese is forced back by the Chinese II/114th, which pushes on to the river. The I/112th envelops the Japanese right flank and captures one of the Japanese positions along the Tarung Hka. At 1700hrs, the I/114th breaks the resistance of the more northerly riverbank fortified positions. After nightfall, a Japanese counterattack from one of the two remaining western riverbank positions fails; this fortified strongpoint is wiped out the following morning.

10. December 29: the remnants of the Japanese defenders on the western riverbank split into small groups. The last Japanese strongpoint along the riverbank holds out until January 13, 1944.

11. December 31: Chinese units of the II/112th trapped to the north in the Sharaw Ga area are relieved by elements of the Chinese 113th Infantry Regiment.

STALEMATE AT YUPBANG GA, OCTOBER 1943–JANUARY 1944

American intelligence officers differed in their estimates of Japanese strength across the Tarung Hka, a common problem that Stilwell would face throughout the entire campaign. One trusted staff officer of Stilwell's thought the Japanese were "awfully strong" while another thought that there were only 400 troops facing the entire Chinese 38th Division. By the end of December 1943, the 38th Division had lost 17 officers and 298 enlisted men killed, and 20 officers and 409 enlisted men wounded. The bulk of the casualties were incurred by the 112th Infantry Regiment.

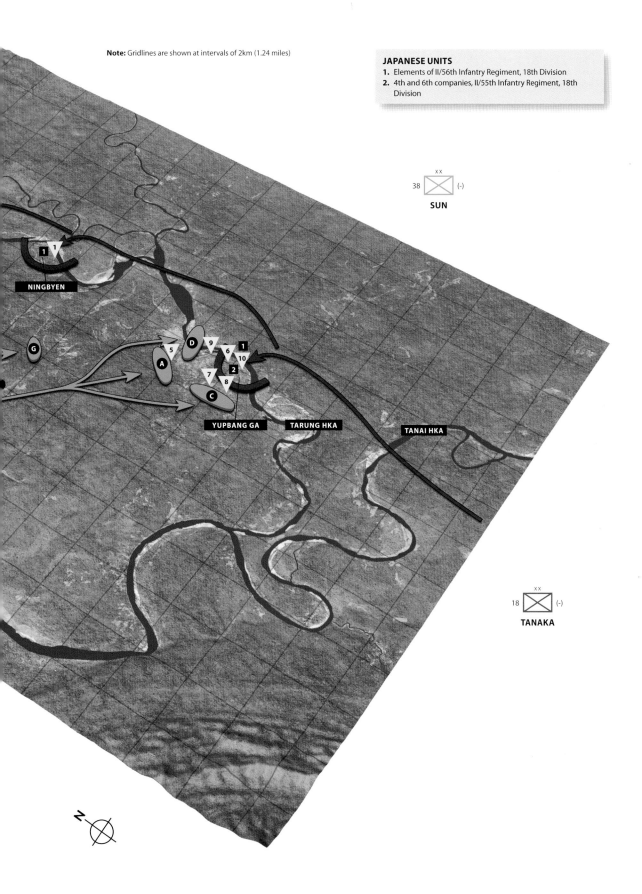

Note: Gridlines are shown at intervals of 2km (1.24 miles)

xx
38 ⊠ (-)
SUN

NINGBYEN

G

D 9
5   6 1
A   10
7 2
8
C

YUPBANG GA   TARUNG HKA   TANAI HKA

xx
18 ⊠ (-)
TANAKA

N

had been fighting for years. Too, after witnessing a spectacular [supply] airdrop of Allied forces the Japanese realized that the fighting power of the American–Chinese forces was not to be underestimated" (quoted in Romanus and Sunderland 1970, p. 127). However, the Japanese still controlled the Tarung crossing at Yupbang Ga.

On December 28 at 1000hrs, the Chinese 1/114th, 2/114th, and the besieged 1/112th attacked again, overcoming some of the Japanese outposts but finding that points of persistent resistance were linked together by tunnels through which the Japanese moved freely. Although the concept of defensive warfare was anathema to the Japanese military mindset, the need to develop fortifications for "retreat combat" became necessary as the fortunes of war shifted. It was only after these extensive tunnels were bypassed that the Chinese were able to get to the Tarung and reduce the other unconnected Japanese positions. The typical Japanese counterattack later that night to regain the lost ground failed, and the remaining strongpoints were reduced on December 29, although the final entrenched fortification was not taken until January 13, 1943, principally due to minefields, which inflicted many Chinese casualties. The surviving Japanese companies split into smaller tactical groups, which managed to continue fighting on for many more days. Finally, the Japanese pulled back across the Tarung, suffering many casualties in the crossing. The besieged Chinese troops to the north at Sharaw Ga were rescued by elements of the Chinese 113th Infantry Regiment on December 31 as the Japanese withdrew. The line of Tanaka's extensive, fortified outposts along the Tarung was now entirely in the hands of the Chinese forces.

The southern part of Stilwell's pincer movement, where the Tarung flows into the Tanai, was tardy. Both the 2/114th and 3/114th crossed Kantau ford in mid-December, but contrary to Stilwell's plan, some of the Chinese companies failed to move forward to envelop elements of the retreating two Japanese regiments north of the Tanai. However, the Chinese 3/114th, broken into small units, confronted the Japanese, in company strength along small tributary creeks (the Sanip and Mawngyang hkas) south of the Tanai Hka; Tanaka's infantry, utilizing their skilled infiltration tactics, slowed Sun Li-jen's progress considerably, impeded his crossing of the Tanai from the south, and almost captured the Chinese 6th Artillery battery prior to the end of the second week of January 1944. It was not until January 29 that Sun Li-jen recommitted the 3/114th with the newly arrived 1/114th to extricate the Japanese dug into the southern bank of the Tanai Hka. The NCAC commander even wondered if Sun Li-jen was disobeying orders by his hesitancy, at the behest of Chiang Kai-shek's intervention. Stilwell's comments reflected his frustration: "Piecemeal action ... Extreme caution and extreme slowness of movement ... Bad recon and security ... Fear of going around ... Result—Loss of men. Loss of chance to bag Japs" (quoted in Romanus and Sunderland 1970, p. 129). The 38th Division's losses by the end of 1943 amounted to 37 officers and 707 enlisted men killed or wounded, but the Ramgarh-trained troops had achieved their first victory in Burma over the Japanese. Stilwell's G-2 reports in the Hukawng Valley gave conflicting reports of both Japanese strength and casualties (Diamond 2013, p. 24), a problem that would become apparent at Myitkyina.

On January 3, 1944 Stilwell ordered Sun Li-jen to advance quickly and capture the village of Taihpa Ga on the Kamaing Road where it crosses the Tanai Hka to the southeast of Yupbang Ga. Typical for Sun Li-jen, his pace was slow, despite having his own artillery. The Japanese strongpoint at Taihpa Ga offered considerable resistance, since it, too, utilized 75mm and 150mm artillery pieces along with well-fortified, entrenched positions. The Japanese held stubbornly to these positions for several weeks. Taihpa Ga was taken on February 1, with the surviving Japanese withdrawing covertly from the area on February 4–5, 1944.

Contemporaneous with the Chinese assault on Taihpa Ga, the Chinese 3/65th Infantry Regiment (22d Division) crossed the Tanai Hka to the west on January 9, and advanced downriver towards Taro on January 30, where it confronted elements of Colonel Yamazaki's 3/55th Infantry Regiment. Also, at Ngajatzup, to the north of the Tanai Hka on the Taro Plain, the 3/112th Chinese infantry were stopped by another battalion of the IJA 55th Infantry Regiment along with ancillary regimental and divisional headquarter units. However, since Tanaka withdrew most of 55th Infantry Regiment to north of the Tanai to reinforce his elements of the 56th Infantry Regiment, which had been defeated at the Tarung Hka fords, Liao Yao-hsiang's 65th Infantry Regiment was eventually able to encircle and overwhelm the now weakened Japanese 3/55th. This cleared the Taro Plain by January 23–25, leading to the capture of Taro on January 30. Liao Yao-hsiang's troops further pursued the survivors of the Taro garrison, trying to reach Tanaka's main body in the Hukawng Valley north of the Tanai Hka, by crossing the Ahawk Hka and marching down the Ahawk Trail across the Wantuk Bum.

In early January 1944, Stilwell requested Wingate to release the 5307th Composite Unit (Provisional) to NCAC operational control for missions in the Hukawng Valley. On January 6, Merrill received command of Galahad with Colonel Charles N. Hunter assigned as his deputy. On January 21–22, Stilwell ordered his 1st Provisional Tank Group, with over 80 tanks, to spearhead a drive down the Kamaing Road, with his Chinese infantry following. Maingkwan, about 15 miles south of Taihpa Ga, was his next objective since it was the main Japanese supply and communication base in the Hukawng Valley. In early February, Stilwell recognized that Sun Li-jen's 38th Division could not carry the infantry lead in the upcoming offensive. The 112th and 114th Infantry regiments' casualty rate exceeded 50 percent and only the 113th was combat ready; however, its performance in the advance to the Tanai had been deemed "slow and cautious." Now, Sun Li-jen's troops would have to follow the 22d Division to the latter's north and east. Thus, on February 4 Stilwell adjusted his forces: "22nd Division, using 65th less one battalion (Taro Garrison) and 66th less one battalion (attached to tanks) was to seize and hold line Yawngbang [Ga]– Lakyen [Ga] sending the 66th past the 114th, and the 65th over the Wantuk Bum ... followed by ... using the tanks and the 65th and 66th, in the hope of getting to Walawbum ... Bad weather had retarded Road work and hampered supply" (quoted in Romanus and Sunderland 1970, p. 143).

Stilwell presents the Silver Star to Colonel Rothwell H. Brown, commander of the 1st Provisional Tank Group, for gallantry and leadership during combat with the IJA 18th Division's 55th and 56th Infantry regiments in the Hukawng Valley, March 1944. (NARA 111-SC-263254)

An American 2½-ton truck with its front wheels almost completely immersed in the muddy quagmire that was once the Kamaing Road. Such conditions severely hampered the progress of the Sino-American advance that Tanaka had hoped for. (USAMHI).

True to his aggressive zeal, Tanaka wanted to renew an offensive up the Hukawng Valley, but Mutaguchi would not permit an offensive that might divert supplies or motor support from his upcoming Imphal offensive, and told him to hold Maingkwan in the center of the valley. Stilwell's 38th and 22d divisions moved slowly down the Hukawng, and came to a halt on January 29. He was going to have to change his tactics in order to descend the Hukawng Valley at a faster rate in order to get to Myitkyina before the monsoon season arrived. Tanaka was already planning that by the time the monsoon rains fell in May or June, he would have created a stalemate near the Jambu Bum ridgeline, which separates the southern end of the Hukawng Valley from the Mogaung Valley. "General Mud" was to be Tanaka's ally. At the Jambu Bum ridgeline, he also had 12 Type 94 75mm mountain guns and four tractor-pulled Type 96 150mm howitzers.

Tanaka had certain advantages in delaying the Sino-American advance. First, he possessed detailed information about the Chinese order of battle. Second, the terrain was more in favor of the defensive force, which would aid him with his numerical disadvantage. The main Kamaing Road could carry wheeled transport only in the dry season, while the large areas of kunai grass served to channel troop movement and also delayed their progress. Due to these terrain features, a Japanese platoon could hold up an entire Chinese battalion. Since Tanaka had observed several times that a serious threat to his flank or rear had come to nothing because the Chinese moved so slowly, he intended to attack the 22d and 38th divisions, defeating each in detail using separate movements. Moreover, as Tanaka retreated, he was shortening his lines of communcation, favoring Japanese resupply, while Stilwell was lengthening his.

A Japanese artillery crew mans its Type 94 (1934) 75mm mountain gun, which most divisional artillery regiments (including the 18th Mountain Artillery Regiment of the 18th Division) were armed with. This gun could be broken down into 11 components for six packhorses to carry. While using the same ammunition as other Japanese 75mm artillery pieces, the range of the Type 94 was only 9,000yd. (NARA 111-SC-135340)

ADVANCE TO WALAWBUM

Having marched from Ledo, the 5307th Composite Unit (Provisional) assembled at Ningbyen near the front between February 19 and 21. The Japanese frontline on February 23 extended from Yawngbang Ga in the southwest across the Hukawng Valley to the vicinity of Warang Ga to the northeast. Due to heavy rains and wet terrain, Stilwell delayed deploying Galahad on their first envelopment mission until late February. The Chinese infantry would advance through the jungle taking Maingkwan frontally, as their tank column cut through jungle trails and drove in on the Japanese lines between Walawbum and Maingkwan. In this, their combat debut, Galahad was to sweep widely to the eastern side of the Hukawng valley, in order to conduct the envelopment of Tanaka's 18th Division, thereby hindering his retreat southwards. Much to Stilwell's chagrin, Yawngbang Ga was not occupied by the Chinese 65th and 66th Infantry regiments until February 23. Even Tanaka commented on the slow movement of the Chinese forces: "If the Chinese 65th and 66th Infantry regiments operating in the vicinity of Yawngbang Ga had been prompt in closing in on our left rear flank on the 15th or 16th [of February], as predicted, the main force of the 18th Division would have faced a grave crisis" (quoted in Romanus and Sunderland 1970, p. 145). Galahad was to create a more rapid offensive tempo in a campaign that had been steadily losing its momentum under Chinese leadership.

From February 23 to March 4, Stilwell advanced on Walawbum, a fire-gutted former Kachin village 12 miles southeast of Maingkwan at the southern end of the Hukawng Valley. Stilwell reasoned that if he could position Galahad just to the east of Walawbum, his American contingent would be in control of high ground with a river, the Numpyek Hka, facing the Japanese to the west. In such a tactical deployment, "Merrill's Marauders" would command the Kamaing Road. With thick, dense vegetation surrounding the clearing at Walawbum, any Japanese unit escaping southwards would be restricted to using narrow trails. Stilwell gave Merrill

The 1st Battalion of the 5307th Composite Unit (Provisional), under the command of Lieutenant-Colonel William L. Osborne, pass in single file and are greeted by Brigadier-General Merrill (left) and Colonel Hunter (far left) at Pangsau Pass on the India–Burma border in February 1944. This unit would shortly receive its moniker "Merrill's Marauders" from a war correspondent. (NARA 559282MM 20)

wide latitude with his verbal orders on February 22 to cut the Japanese supply line using the Kamaing Road well to the south.

On February 24, the three Marauder battalions began their trek in columns of combat teams, with their Intelligence and Reconnaissance (I&R) platoons in the lead. After skirmishing with many Japanese patrols, Merrill directed his combat teams farther to the east. In Merrill's favor, signals communications between IJA 18th Division headquarters and 2/56th Infantry Regiment was nonfunctional for a time, which meant Tanaka was unaware of the American flanking movement. On February 28, a liaison aircraft brought orders to Merrill to shift the roadblock site to Walawbum itself.

On March 2, after marching roughly 40 miles and crossing three formidable streams, the Marauders approached Walawbum. Initially, Merrill wanted to position his battalions at the Nambyu Hka, well to the west of Walawbum, but Stilwell was confident that the Chinese-American armor could get to the river line there and hold it. The 3d Battalion, under Lieutenant-Colonel Charles Beach, was assigned the high ground just to the east of Walawbum, covering the Kamaing Road with his heavy weapons platoons, on the eastern bank of the Numpyek Hka. The 2d Battalion, under Lieutenant-Colonel George McGee, went across the river and set up a blocking position on the Kamaing Road just over 2 miles to the west of Walawbum. The 1st Battalion, under Osborne, was split up with one combat team being held in reserve by Merrill, while the other had some of its troops deployed in machine-gun emplacement blocks north of the Kamaing Road on the trails in the vicinity of Sana Ga that led to Walawbum, as Japanese troops were trying to escape south to the village to avoid the steady advance of the Chinese 113th Infantry Regiment in the wake of Merrill's battalions. Other elements of the 1st Battalion were actively patrolling along the Numpyek Hka.

Tanaka was made aware of the American thrust towards Walawbum on March 1 after radio communications were restored. Leaving a small rearguard against the slowly advancing Chinese infantry, he sent the 55th Infantry Regiment to strike Galahad on its northern flank while the 56th Infantry Regiment moved beyond where the Kamaing Road crosses the Nambyu Hka. On March 3, the Japanese made probing attacks against 3d Battalion's I&R platoon, under the command of Lieutenant

A Marauder patrol of the 3d Battalion, under the command of Lieutenant-Colonel Charles E. Beach, treks through a path in the jungle in the Walawbum area in early March 1944. (NARA 559282 MM 34)

Allied advance in the Hukawng Valley and Marauder assault on Walawbum

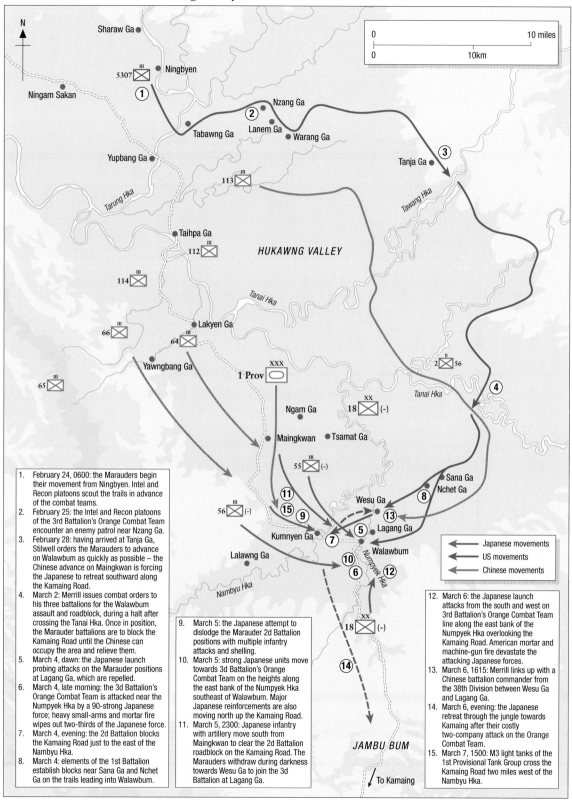

N

Sharaw Ga

Ningbyen

5307

①

Ningam Sakan

Nzang Ga

②

Lanem Ga

Tabawng Ga

Warang Ga

③

Yupbang Ga

Tanja Ga

Tarung Hka

113

Tawang Hka

Taihpa Ga

112

HUKAWNG VALLEY

114

Tanai Hka

Lakyen Ga

66

64

2 56

Yawngbang Ga

XXX

1 Prov

Tanai Hka

④

65

Ngam Ga

XX

18 (-)

Maingkwan

Tsamat Ga

55 (-)

Sana Ga

Nchet Ga

⑪

Wesu Ga

⑧

56 (-)

⑮

⑨

⑬

Kumnyen Ga

⑤

Lagang Ga

⑦

Walawbum

Lalawng Ga

⑩

Numpyek Hka

⑥

⑫

Nambyu Hka

XX

18 (-)

⑭

JAMBU BUM

To Kamaing

1. February 24, 0600: the Marauders begin their movement from Ningbyen. Intel and Recon platoons scout the trails in advance of the combat teams.
2. February 25: the Intel and Recon platoons of the 3rd Battalion's Orange Combat Team encounter an enemy patrol near Nzang Ga.
3. February 28: having arrived at Tanja Ga, Stilwell orders the Marauders to advance on Walawbum as quickly as possible – the Chinese advance on Maingkwan is forcing the Japanese to retreat southward along the Kamaing Road.
4. March 2: Merrill issues combat orders to his three battalions for the Walawbum assault and roadblock, during a halt after crossing the Tanai Hka. Once in position, the Marauder battalions are to block the Kamaing Road until the Chinese can occupy the area and relieve them.
5. March 4, dawn: the Japanese launch probing attacks on the Marauder positions at Lagang Ga, which are repelled.
6. March 4, late morning: the 3d Battalion's Orange Combat Team is attacked near the Numpyek Hka by a 90-strong Japanese force; heavy small-arms and mortar fire wipes out two-thirds of the Japanese force.
7. March 4, evening: the 2d Battalion blocks the Kamaing Road just to the east of the Nambyu Hka.
8. March 4: elements of the 1st Battalion establish blocks near Sana Ga and Nchet Ga on the trails leading into Walawbum.

9. March 5: the Japanese attempt to dislodge the Marauder 2d Battalion positions with multiple infantry attacks and shelling.
10. March 5: strong Japanese units move towards 3d Battalion's Orange Combat Team on the heights along the east bank of the Numpyek Hka southeast of Walawbum. Major Japanese reinforcements are also moving north up the Kamaing Road.
11. March 5, 2300: Japanese infantry with artillery move south from Maingkwan to clear the 2d Battalion roadblock on the Kamaing Road. The Marauders withdraw during darkness towards Wesu Ga to join the 3d Battalion at Lagang Ga.

12. March 6: the Japanese launch attacks from the south and west on 3rd Battalion's Orange Combat Team line along the east bank of the Numpyek Hka overlooking the Kamaing Road. American mortar and machine-gun fire devastate the attacking Japanese forces.
13. March 6, 1615: Merrill links up with a Chinese battalion commander from the 38th Division between Wesu Ga and Lagang Ga.
14. March 6, evening: the Japanese retreat through the jungle towards Kamaing after their costly two-company attack on the Orange Combat Team.
15. March 7, 1500: M3 light tanks of the 1st Provisional Tank Group cross the Kamaing Road two miles west of the Nambyu Hka.

0 —————————— 10 miles
0 —————————— 10km

Japanese movements
US movements
Chinese movements

Logan Weston, to the west of the Numpyek Hka. They also struck Orange Combat Team of 3d Battalion, which was now well entrenched, in large part due to the diversion created by its I&R platoon, to withstand the Japanese 56th Infantry Regiment's mortar and 75mm artillery rounds on the east side of the Numpyek Hka after setting up their heavy weapons. Other elements of the 3d Battalion clashed with the Japanese throughout March 3, and its Khaki Combat Team stayed at Lagang Ga, an air-supply drop zone, after killing 30 Japanese who tried to seize it. The same drop zone was attacked the next morning by the Japanese, under cover of early morning mist and from broken ground. Again, the Americans of Khaki Combat Team held the liaison plane airfield, killing ten enemy infantrymen in the attack; a further seven were killed when six soldiers carrying a wounded Japanese officer stumbled on their retreat into the Marauders' 3d Battalion command post close to the airstrip.

The 56th Infantry Regiment tried to cross the Numpyek Hka on March 4 to get around the 3d Battalion's flanks, but ambushes and "booby traps" alerted the defenders. Japanese troops did get to the east side of the river, but over 75 Japanese dead were later counted for one Marauder killed and seven wounded. The Japanese tried to organize attacks during March 5, but accurate 81mm mortar fire and P-51 Mustang air attacks broke up troop concentrations. However, amid increasing pressure while repelling five separate Japanese attacks from the northerly direction between 0730 and 1100hrs on March 5, and with low ammunition reserves, the 3d Battalion's I&R platoon had to withdraw across the Numpyek Hka under mortar and machine-gun supportive fire from its Khaki Combat Team. Suffering two wounded Marauders, Weston's I&R platoon inflicted an estimated two-thirds casualties on the attacking Japanese force of roughly 90 infantrymen.

Tanaka claimed after the war that his 3/56th captured the Nambyu Hka crossing with one rapid attack on March 4, which differs from American accounts (quoted in Romanus and Sunderland 1970, p. 152). Early on March 5, small groups of Japanese soldiers moving along the Kamaing Road to the west of Walawbum were wiped out by the machine-gun fire from 2d Battalion's roadblocks that had been established the previous evening. In those positions, the 2d Battalion's Blue Combat Team fought off repeated Japanese attacks and was under greater pressure due to its proximity to the main Japanese troop concentrations of the 56th Infantry Regiment. Green Combat Team's roadblocks were facing east back towards the village of Walawbum. After over 36 hours of holding the block, and now with no food or water and with ammunition running out, the 2d Battalion was ordered to withdraw from its roadblock to the northwest across the Numpyek Hka to Wesu Ga, to the north of Lagang Ga, for resupply on March 5. Colonel McGee's men made it back to Wesu Ga during the afternoon of March 6 and then, according to plan, headed off to rejoin the 3d Battalion just to the south of Walawbum.

On March 3, the Chinese infantry and armored advance began roughly three miles to the north of Maingkwan; by March 6, Liao Yao-hsiang's 22d Division and Brown's 1st Provisional Tank Group had captured the town. After taking Maingkwan, the Chinese 66th Infantry Regiment, along with elements of the 64th Infantry Regiment, advanced south down the Kamaing Road and attacked Japanese entrenchments on March 4–5 near Kumnyen Ga to the west of Walawbum. The Chinese–American armor was to cross the Nambyu Hka and headed for Walawbum. On the morning of March 5, after some heavy going to the north and west of where the 2d Battalion and

Orange Combat Team's I&R platoon had been fighting, Brown's tankers broke through into a Japanese bivouac area, which turned out to be Tanaka's division and the 56th regimental headquarters, and engaged a body of Japanese in company strength. Also, the Chinese–American tankers had come down a trail that the 55th Infantry Regiment was to have used to attack Galahad. Due to the presence of enemy armor along its marching route, the path of the 55th Infantry Regiment had been shifted to the west and was actually behind the 56th Infantry Regiment on column instead of astride it or in echelon for an assault on Galahad. At roughly 1600hrs on March 6, Brown's tankers met Merrill at Wesu Ga.

Coupled with the absence of a breakthrough against Galahad by the Japanese 56th Infantry Regiment, Tanaka decided to circumvent the 2d Battalion's roadblock on the Kamaing Road by using a secret track that his engineers had very recently constructed in order to re-establish his forces further south across the Kamaing Road, in an east–west position facing the Americans and Chinese to the north. The roughly 12½-mile trail was constructed by Colonel Fukayama of the Engineer Regiment on his own initiative as he became concerned about the reversals in the Japanese position at Walawbum. The jungle trail led from the vicinity of Lalawng Ga to Jambu Hkintang; 18th Division used it to withdraw its main body from the engagement at Walawbum. Late on March 5, orders were given via a field telephone by one of Tanaka's staff to put the retreat plan into effect. This conversation was intercepted by Sergeant Roy H. Matsumoto, a Nisei

An M3 light tank, with a Sino-American crew, attached to one of Stilwell's Chinese divisions, meets with elements of Merrill's Marauders after the victory at Walawbum. This would be the only time that the 5307th Composite Unit (Provisional) would interact with the armored force. (NARA 559282 MM 12)

1ST PROVISIONAL TANK GROUP UNDER ATTACK AT WALAWBUM, MARCH 3–4, 1944 (PP. 52–53)

A Chinese M3A3 light-tank commander (**1**), of the 3d Company, 1st Battalion, 1st Provisional Tank Group, is about to pull down the hatch of his vehicle as it wheels off a jungle track into thick, tall grass to attack a camouflaged Japanese 37mm Type 94 rapid-fire infantry gun (**2**) used in an antitank role at Wesu Ga, just to the northwest of Walawbum. The M3 light tank to the left (**3**) is in flames from a hit scored a moment before.

The small Burmese village of Walawbum is situated on the Kamaing Road directly across from the Numpyek Hka. There were numerous access trails that fed into the main Kamaing Road, one of which the M3A3 light tanks were motoring down when they came under fire from the enemy's antitank gun. The muddy access trails were strewn with grass stems from the surrounding dense, tall fields of kunai or "elephant" grass ranging as high as 12 to 15ft. Copses of tall verdant trees were sporadically situated along the access trail. The banks of the Hka had low, heavily forested areas. Thus, in addition to booby traps that could be placed along the access trail, the locale was a perfect place for a camouflaged Japanese ambush site.

Elements of two Japanese infantry regiments (the 55th and 56th) of Tanaka's 18th Division had disengaged from the Chinese infantry, slowly moving from the northwest to combat the Americans of the 5307th Composite Unit (Provisional) and reconnaissance M3A3 light tanks of the 1st Provisional Tank Group. Japanese troops were feverishly moving around the areas where the Marauder battalions had set up their roadblocks and positions near Walawbum, as Hunter was trying to rendezvous with Rothwell Brown's Chinese and attached American tankers.

The Japanese knew that the tanks had to stay on the narrow roads because of the jungle and tall kunai grass.

According to one Marauder's account (that of Charlton Ogburn), "To our stupefaction we came upon a tank at Wesu Ga. It squatted on the trail, indolently powerful, making harsh, rumbling noises in its depth while its Chinese crew lolled at leisure, looking careworn but entirely at home with the monster. The last vehicle of any kind we had seen was a two-week march to the rear, and I had not known there were tanks of any kind on our side in Burma" (Ogburn, C., *The Marauders*, Quill: New York, 1982, p. 124). The Marauders had previously been hit by flat-trajectory shelling, which was proof that the Japanese had in fact been moving in artillery. American tankers attached to the Chinese had frequently documented elements of the Japanese 18th Division hiding in the tall elephant grass in ambush positions.

The Japanese lightweight 37mm Type 94 artillery gun was a derivative of the German Pak 35/36, and it served as the main Japanese AT gun. The Type 94 number was designated for the year the gun was accepted, 2594 in the Japanese imperial year calendar or 1934 in the Gregorian calendar. The gun was introduced in 1936 for service in the Sino-Japanese War. Type 94 37mm AT guns were typically assigned in groups of four to combat infantry regiments. Each gun was manned by a squad of 11 personnel, and was kept in contact with the regimental headquarters by either field telephone or messenger runner. Its effective firing rang was just over 3,100yd. The gun remained in service on most fronts in World War Two for lack of a better replacement.

interpreter in the 2d Battalion. In a matter of minutes, Merrill and his subordinates knew of Tanaka's escape plan and route. Serendipitously, on the afternoon of March 7, one of Brown's tank columns may have found Fukayama's trail as it turned off the Kamaing Road on the west side of the Nambyu Hka; they found a track exhibiting heavy troop movement. Soon thereafter, the tankers found a body of Japanese on the march and sent them fleeing. Two weeks later, 200 Japanese bodies were found in a common grave at that site where the tanks had been.

At 1715hrs on March 6, roughly two companies of Japanese skirmishers in extended formation following each other, under the cover of their artillery fire, crossed the Numpyek Hka. Their officers exhorted their troops, by waving their samurai swords, to attack the dug-in positions of the 3d Marauder Battalion's Orange Combat Team on the eastern bank. Except for the Marauders' mortar bombardment, the Americans did not open fire until the Japanese were within 40yd. Then, Marauder heavy machine guns, with a clear field of fire, tore into the shouting Japanese, killing many both on the open ground on the east side of the Numpyek Hka and at the riverbank during the 45-minute engagement. An estimated 400 Japanese infantrymen were killed or left dying in this *banzai* charge across the Numpyek Hka for the cost of only a handful of Marauders wounded. This was the bloodiest fighting of the Marauders' first mission.

Tanaka's decision to withdraw down the secretly constructed jungle trail was timely, as leading elements of Sun Li-jen's 113th Infantry Regiment, which had been following Merrill's battalions, met the Americans at Wesu Ga, northeast of Walawbum, at 1600hrs on March 6. Unfortunately, there was a "friendly fire" encounter on March 7 in which a few Chinese infantrymen were wounded. Now that the Chinese were on the battlefield, later that day Merrill ordered Galahad, over the protests of his battalion commanders, to circle south and recut the Kamaing Road farther to the south, which essentially removed the Marauders from any further combat near Walawbum. Apart from the movements by Brown's tanks, with sporadic fire from some Japanese 37mm antitank guns, the battle was over, as the tanks and elements of the 38th Division joined up at the burned-out village of Walawbum. The escape of the major body of 18th Division irked Stilwell, but his Allied forces now controlled the larger part of the Hukawng Valley with its victory over the Japanese at Walawbum. The battle had raged for five days from March 4 to 8, and Tanaka's division suffered an estimated 800 dead for only eight Marauders killed and 37 wounded. An additional 179 Marauders were evacuated because of injuries and sickness. This part of the campaign heralded a war of movement, which was quite different to the two-month stalemate at the Tarung–Tanai outposts near Yupbang Ga. However, on March 15, Tanaka dug in on the Jambu Bum at the southern end of the Hukawng Valley.

A Chinese M3 light tank of the 3d Company, 1st Provisional Tank Group moves up a road, having been in contact with Japanese artillery and mortar fire throughout the entire previous night near Walawbum, on March 4, 1944. The M3's armament comprised a 37mm gun and two 7.7mm machine guns. Its armor was much thicker than its Japanese counterparts at between 15 and 43mm. (NARA 111-SC-263248)

INTO THE MOGAUNG VALLEY

Shaduzup

The next stage of Stilwell's northern Burma campaign was to gain control of the Mogaung Valley. In order to accomplish this, the Japanese infantry and artillery would have to be forced off the Jambu Bum separating the Hukawng from the Mogaung valleys. Stilwell ordered Galahad to make a pair of envelopments. Their trek commenced on March 12 from Sana Ga. The Marauder 1st Battalion, with the Chinese 38th Division's 113th Infantry Regiment following it, would conduct the more shallow "hook" to block the Kamaing Road, the main Japanese line of communication, at Shaduzup, which was located to the south of the Jambu Bum. Then, the 2d and 3rd Marauder battalions would execute the wider of the two envelopments and establish a roadblock near the village of Inkangahtawng, roughly eight miles further south of Shaduzup along the Kamaing Road. This wider "hook" would necessitate an approximately 80-mile circuitous trek across the steep western slopes of the Kumon Range and would represent a new challenge for the Marauders and their pack animals. Once across the western face of the Kumon Range, the 2d and 3rd battalions would then encounter additional rough terrain through the constricted valley formed by the Tanai Hka and the two main chains of the mountain range, where elevation could change precipitously. This arduous march paralleled the Kamaing Road roughly 12 miles to the east at the level of Walawbum. The intent that Stilwell had for both of these enveloping maneuvers was for the Marauders to reach their tactical destinations after about two weeks, strike simultaneously by establishing two separate roadblocks in order to pinch out the Japanese between these positions, and then to attack north or south along the Kamaing Road or in both directions, as dictated by the enemy response.

A Kachin teenage boy and an American Marauder, both armed with M1928 Thompson .45-cal. submachine guns, survey the fields of fire around Myitkyina. The Thompson was an ideal personal weapon here; it provided heavy, mobile fire to suppress enemy positions while other infantry approached with grenades, rifle fire, flamethrowers or satchel charges to reduce them. (NARA 559282 MM 215)

The Marauder 1st Battalion, led by Lieutenant-Colonel William Osborne, along with the Chinese 113th Infantry Regiment and the 6th Pack Artillery Battery, began their 50-mile "narrow hook" march. Osborne's battalion followed a trail running through the southeastern end of the Hukawng Valley and along the southwestern slopes of the Kumon Range to the Mogaung Valley. On March 14, the I&R platoon of White Combat Team, south of Makuy Bum and several miles in front of the main column, stumbled into a small group of Japanese soldiers in bivouac. A handful of Japanese were killed; however, this alerted a further 150 Japanese and the platoon quickly dispersed into the jungle. An additional rifle platoon from the main body, along with Red Combat Team's I&R platoon, arrived to help drive the enemy across the nearby Numpyek Hka. On the following day, the main column had eight separate skirmishes with small parties of patrolling Japanese infantry.

Unknown to Osborne and his force, a considerable amount of assistance was being given to them by a group of Kachin guerrillas led by Lieutenant James Tilly of Detachment 101 of the OSS. This Kachin force was delegated to Merrill's command to gather military intelligence, and furnish information about roads and trails as well as ambush and harass the rear of the Japanese forces during this trek. The Kachin operation here kept the enemy from moving east to west to combat the Marauders, but also inflicted considerable casualties on the Japanese. Osborne, in order to get to his intended position at Shaduzup on schedule with those of the other Marauder battalions arriving at their targets, decided to cut a trail through the jungle towards Kumshan Ga on March 16 with the White Combat Team to get around the Japanese force that he and the Kachins had been confronting. It took two days, with every member of White Combat Team using their machetes and Gurkha kukris, to hack a trail to Kumshan Ga by March 17, a distance of only four miles. The next day, Osborne's troops were resupplied by an airdrop in a mountain clearing that had been turned into a drop zone. On the night of March 18, the 1st Battalion made contact with the 50 Kachins under Tilly near Jaiwa Ga. Kachin guides would now escort Osborne's force the remainder of the march to Shaduzup. Although trying to minimize contact with the enemy to preserve an element of surprise for the construction of the roadblock at Shaduzup, small firefights on enemy-guarded trails on March 20–21 compelled Osborne to cut a new cross-country path southwards. From March 23–24, during a five-mile bamboo hacking march, no Japanese troops were encountered. The main battalion column was to proceed down the Chengun Hka, a tributary of the Mogaung River, to reach their destination of the Kamaing Road. On the night of March 26, the 1st Battalion arrived at the upper reaches of the Chengun Hka and waded downstream to within a mile of their objective.

An American signaler taps on the Morse key on his wireless system to communicate both with field units in the vicinity of Myitkyina as well as approaching aircraft and rear echelon areas. Tents were erected to the sides of the airstrip's runway for both medical purposes as well as to keep the radio equipment as dry as possible; in the wet, humid environment of Burma, corrosion of components was a constant problem. Prior to Mogaung's fall at the end of June, Stilwell's Sino-American force was surrounded and dependent solely on air supply. (USAMHI)

The Chinese–American force had insinuated itself stealthily during the night of March 27/28. At Shaduzup, the Japanese had 300 troops and there were 500–600 more in the vicinity of Jambu Bum to the north. White Combat Team's I&R platoon found an enemy camp between the Mogaung River and the Kamaing Road, with at least one Japanese company there and another at a larger camp a short distance to the south. Osborne planned to attack the northern Japanese camp at dawn on March 28 with three columns from White Combat Team. Another set of three Marauder columns would be ready for flanking movements or to deal with an enemy force coming up from the southern camp. The Chinese infantry and artillery were held in reserve. The Marauders overran the first Japanese camp and set up a roadblock on the Kamaing Road; under Japanese artillery fire, which began at 1000hrs, the Marauders held it against counterattacks from all directions, and inflicted extensive casualties on the enemy. The Japanese assaults tapered off by the late afternoon, but artillery shelling continued. Since the Marauders had no artillery in place yet, they fired their mortars and used hand grenades until Chinese infantry with pack artillery relieved them just before dawn on March 29.

The same day, elements of the IJA 18th Division at Shaduzup initially withdrew to the southwest not only to break contact with the Chinese 64th Infantry Regiment, which was four miles to the north coming down the Kamaing Road from Walawbum towards Jambu Bum, but to bypass the Marauder 1st Battalion block on the Kamaing road, which had cost them 300 men killed. At 1500hrs, patrols from a battalion of the Chinese 113th Infantry Regiment, in pursuit of the retreating Japanese, met their counterparts from the 64th Infantry Regiment at Laban. The Hukawng–Mogaung corridor and the Kamaing Road were now open to Laban, approximately one mile to the south of the roadblock.

Osborne had been previously ordered by Merrill to leave the roadblock after his mission was completed and the Chinese were in position. The 1st Battalion was then to march in a southeastwardly direction to rejoin the remaining two 5307th battalions, in the vicinity of Hsamshingyang. Although the 2d and 3d Marauder battalions would subsequently become engaged in a major battle with the Japanese at Nhpum Ga, it would not be until April 7 that Osborne's 1st Battalion would arrive to assist the other two battalions. From April 1–3, the 1st Battalion would be out of contact with Merrill's headquarters, due to the destruction of the unit's only long-range radio – an errant grain sack landed on it after free-falling from a supply aircraft. Once radio communication was re-established on April 3, Merrill directed the 1st Battalion to Hsamshingyang with the greatest speed.

Kachin scouts follow a Marauder point man as a column advances down an unknown track through the Kumon Range for the *coup de main* attack on the western airfield at Myitkyina in mid-May 1944. These local Burmese natives were invaluable to the success of the mission. (USAMHI)

Inkangahtawng and Nhpum Ga

Galahad's 2d and 3d battalions also left Sana Ga, north of Walawbum, on March 12, and trekked in a two-column march down the east side of the Hukawng Valley from March 12 to 14. The Chinese regiment that was scheduled to accompany this column was not available to follow the Marauder columns on March 12. On March 15, at the village of Naubum, the Marauder column was met by Captain Vincent Curl and 300 Kachin guerrillas of Detachment 101. Both battalions, with their Kachin escort, moved through the Kumon hills from March 15 to 21, and on the 23rd they arrived further south of Shaduzup on the Kamaing Road at the village of Inkangahtawng to establish a roadblock there. By placing his Marauders well to the south of Shaduzup, Stilwell intended to seal off the entrance to Mogaung Valley and effectively prohibit overland supply, thereby producing a severance of the Japanese 18th Division's headquarters at Myitkyina in the Irrawaddy Valley from the northern Hukawng–Mogaung Valley corridor. Stilwell had studied the geography and knew the transportation routes through the Burmese river valleys. Through careful intelligence and planning, he knew that the Mogaung Valley was the vital link between Myitkyina in the Irrawaddy Valley and the most northward forward elements of Tanaka's 18th Division. The Japanese also realized the significance of Stilwell's attacks and were determined to prevent him from reaching Kamaing to the southwest of Inkangahtawng. Furthermore, Tanaka was aware that with Stilwell in possession of Kamaing, he would be a potential threat to the upcoming Japanese assault on the British garrison at Imphal, Operation *U-Go*, as well as to his 18th Division's lines of communication. Stilwell's intelligence officers believed that the Japanese infantry were about 2,000 strong to the south and west of Kamaing.

Elements of the 5307th's 2d Battalion encountered and clashed with the Japanese on March 23, the latter in company strength and dug in at Inkangahtawng. The Marauders had arrived well ahead of schedule, on Merrill's orders, since the Chinese 22d Division had taken Jambu Bum. Now the Japanese were alerted to the American presence and the Marauder commanders suspected that enemy reinforcements would now be sent to Inkangahtawng. The next day, March 24, McGee sent two reinforced Marauder platoons to surround the village of Inkangahtawng; however, they had to withdraw after finding it too strongly defended with fortified Japanese entrenchments. Japanese reinforcements were hastily dispatched to the south from the 18th Division's headquarters at Shaduzup, as Osborne's 1st Battalion was not to attack this more northerly garrison until dawn on March 28. Later on March 24, the 2nd Battalion's left flank was heavily attacked with the Japanese suffering numerous casualties. The heavy American defensive fire caused a shortage in ammunition. Made aware that two Japanese battalions were converging upon them, McGee ordered his 2d Battalion to retreat from the Kamaing roadblock at Inkangahtawng and cross the Mogaung River to Ngagahtawng, in order to limit its losses. The roadblock had been held for 24 hours, causing the Marauders to lose two killed and 12 wounded. The Japanese dead exceeded 200 infantrymen. Tanaka had reacted swiftly and decisively to prevent the blockade of the Kamaing Road at Inkangahtawng by counterattacking on 24 March with a 1,600-man force comprising the 1/55th Infantry Regiment with two companies of the 114th Infantry Regiment. His intent was to get around the

The drive across the Jambu Bum to attack the IJA 18th Division

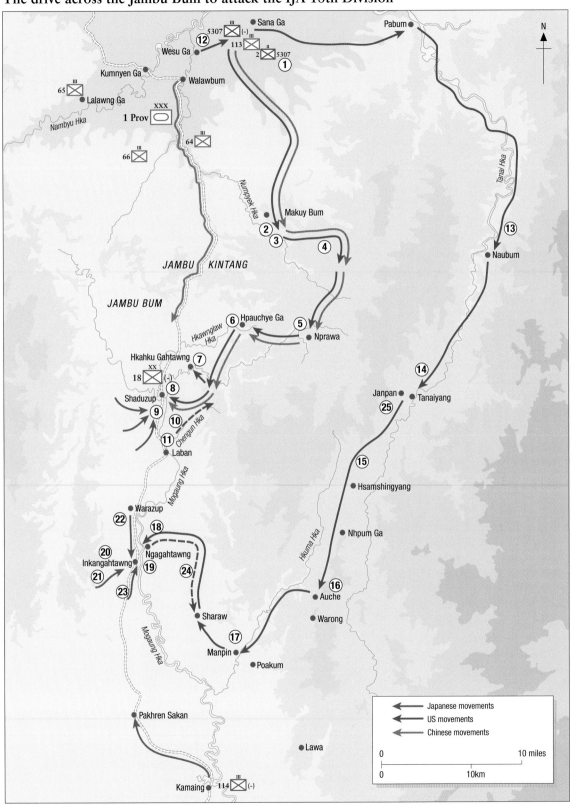

1st Battalion, 5307th Composite Unit (Provisional)

1. March 12, 0700hrs: the 1st Battalion, 5307th Composite, followed by the Chinese 113th Infantry Regiment, 38th Division, and the 6th Pack Artillery Battery, start their trek towards Shaduzup on the "narrow envelopment" from Sana Ga.
2. March 14: I&R Platoon, White Combat Team (1st Battalion), engages 150 Japanese in a firefight on a trail south of Makuy Bum, forcing the Japanese across the nearby Numpyek Hka.
3. March 15: 1st Battalion engages in eight separate skirmishes over the subsequent 1–2 miles.
4. March 16: to avoid further delays, Osborne orders White Combat Team to carve a shortcut trail east; it takes them two days to cut a four-mile trail through the vegetation.
5. March 20: having made contact with Tilly's Kachins, the Marauders stumble into a firefight with a Japanese machine-gun position at the village of Nprawa.
6. March 21: the advance platoon of Red Combat Team secures Japanese entrenchments at Hpauchye Ga. Osborne decides to cut another path south towards the Chengun Hka, which takes two days to complete.
7. March 25: Osborne sends one rifle platoon as a feint to Hkahku Gahtawng to deceive the enemy that Shaduzup is going to be attacked from the northeast.
8. March 26: the main body of 1st Battalion arrives at Shaduzup.
9. March 28, 0300hrs: Osborne launches a surprise night attack on the Japanese camp, achieving complete surprise. Japanese attempts to retake the position continue for the rest of the day.
10. March 29, before dawn: the Chinese 113th Infantry Regiment and 6th Pack Artillery Battery take over the roadblock perimeter and Red Combat Team's positions to the east of the Mogaung Hka.
11. March 29: 1st Battalion withdraws one mile up the Chengun Hka, and is ordered to proceed to Janpan and then Hsamshingyang. The Chinese 22d Division regiments make progress against slackening Japanese resistance, and the Kamaing Road is declared open to Laban.

2d and 3d battalions, 5307th Composite Unit (Provisional)

12. March 12, 0700hrs: 2d Battalion leaves Wesu Ga and heads for Pabum followed by the command group and the 3d Battalion.
13. March 15: the 2d and 3d battalions reach Naubum and meet Curl's Detachment 101 with 300 Kachin guerrillas.
14. March 16: the 2d and 3d battalions arrive at Tanaiyang, where they clear a field for a food air-supply drop.
15. March 16–21: 2d Battalion, Khaki Combat Team of the 3d Battalion, and Kachin guides, under Hunter, head southwest towards Warong; Orange Combat Team of the 3d Battalion remains at Janpan with Merrill's headquarters.
16. March 22: at Auche, Hunter is ordered to push on towards the Kamaing Road ahead of schedule as the Japanese are withdrawing south along the road.
17. March 23: Hunter's force heads to Manpin and from there through Sharaw into the Mogaung Valley.
18. March 23: 2d Battalion patrols clash with a company of Japanese troops near Inkangahtawng.
19. March 23: Khaki Combat Team, 3d Battalion, moves to a position on the east bank of the Mogaung Hka to provide protective mortar fire to 2d Battalion.
20. March 24, dawn: McGee sends two reinforced platoons of his 2d Battalion to envelope Inkangahtawng from west to east, but his troops are forced to withdraw.
21. March 24, 0700hrs: 2d Battalion's left flank comes under heavy attack from the west of the Kamaing Road; the attack is repulsed.
22. March 24, 1000hrs: Japanese attacks from the north from the vicinity of Warazup are repulsed.
23. March 24, afternoon: Japanese troops assault the perimeter from the south once again supported by mortar, machine-gun and artillery fire.
24. March 24, 1630hrs: McGee decides to withdraw towards Manpin. Hunter, at Sharaw to the south, is unaware of the withdrawal from Inkangahtawng.
25. Merrill learns that a strong enemy force of two battalions is on the move from Kamaing to the Tanai Hka Valley with orders to advance north in that area, and then turn westward to attack the flank of the Chinese 22d Division near Shaduzup. Stilwell orders Merrill to block this move and prevent any Japanese advance beyond Nhpum Ga.

Marauders' flank then head north into the Tanai River valley and finally turn westward to attack the flank of the Chinese 22d Division. Stilwell ordered Merrill to block this northward Japanese thrust and prevent any enemy advance beyond Nhpum Ga, which was located astride a ridgeline of the Kumon Range that was deemed to be desirable terrain.

On March 26, the Marauders' 2d and 3d battalions, under Charles Hunter's combined command, learned from Merrill that about two additional understrength battalions of roughly 800 Japanese troops were moving northeast from Kamaing towards Nhpum Ga to protect Tanaka's right flank and perhaps isolate the Marauders as they moved east from Inkangahtawng. Fighting rearguard actions against these Japanese reinforcements from Kamaing, Galahad delayed the enemy movement towards Nhpum Ga from March 26 to 28. According to the official US history, "The main body of the 2nd and 3rd battalions kept moving northwards away from Kamaing with the former setting up a defensive perimeter at Nhpum Ga on 28 March while Merrill placed the 3rd Battalion on a course moving northwards towards a clearing in the jungle, Hsamshingyang, to protect an airstrip there for evacuation and re-supply" (Romanus and Sunderland 1970, p. 188). After the war, Hunter wrote: "it seemed to me … the important installation of Kamaing must now be wide open; and here I sat with a battalion and a half of troops just five or six miles away. I radioed Merrill for permission to move in on the place; it would be a bigger coup than our now abandoned

Lieutenant-Colonel Charles E. Beach (left), commanding officer 3d Battalion, greets Lieutenant-Colonel George A. McGee, Jr., commanding officer 2d Battalion, on April 9, 1944 at Hsamshingyang after the siege of Nhpum Ga was raised. (NARA 559282 MM 207)

A Marauder scoops water with his mess tin cup into a plastic bag for chlorination. Troops on both sides had to be ever vigilant to purify their water before drinking to avoid dysentery and cholera. Despite the best of efforts, these diseases often reduced the ranks of the fighting troops and severely debilitated them in combat. (NARA 559282 MM 126)

Inkangahtawng project and would cut off the rear of the Japanese forces we had been ordered to intercept at Auche. To my disappointment I was told to withdraw; I still believe it was a golden opportunity that should have been exploited" (Hunter 1993, p. 8).

On March 27, with 3d Battalion covering their movement, 2d Battalion moved onto Auche. The 3d Battalion would eventually clear Nhpum Ga and proceed to the Hsamshingyang area, with its airstrip, about five miles north of Nhpum Ga. By 1200hrs on March 28, the perimeter was set by McGee's 2d Battalion at Nhpum Ga. On the following day, Merrill suffered a heart attack, his second since he had been in Southeast Asia, and was evacuated. The Japanese attacked Nhpum Ga in force on March 30. The roughly 200 x 400yd perimeter held despite severe attacks and McGee strongly urged Hunter, now in command of Galahad, to keep open the trail from Nhpum Ga to Hsamshingyang. A detachment of the Japanese 114th Infantry Regiment, led by Colonel Maruyama Fusayasu, took a water point from the Marauders on March 30. The 2d Battalion thus became short of water. By nightfall on March 30, it was evident that the Japanese were digging in for a siege of the Nhpum Ga perimeter. Repeated heavy assaults supported by Japanese artillery and mortar fire from March 31 to April 2 caused mounting casualties in the 2d Battalion. Hunter ordered McGee to fight his way out of the Japanese encirclement to the northwest on April 3; however, the next day McGee stressed the impossibility of the situation, especially to the north. On April 5, 2d Battalion received more of the same from the Japanese although initially not as severe as the previous day. No supply drop of water would occur; the 5307th was not trained for air resupply operations of water. That evening, the Japanese launched a series of violent assaults and suffered heavy losses. On April 6 water came, although insufficient to meet the battalion's needs, causing the senior surgeon there to question whether he should use the water for drinking or making casts. The fighting would rage on at Nhpum Ga until April 9.

The 2d Battalion lived a day-to-day existence, with air resupply their only source of relief. When Hunter was unable to break into the perimeter with 3d Battalion from Hsamshingyang, he had the "strength of purpose" to redirect Osborne's 1st Battalion, retreating from Shaduzup, to Nhpum Ga; the unit arrived on Easter Sunday, April 7.

An airdrop at Janpan, a Kachin village, on March 19, 1944. The village was used as a drop marker since there was no suitable clearing on any of the nearby rugged mountains. (NARA 559282 MM 64)

Exemplifying Hunter's leadership caliber and character, he told his 3d Battalion as they pushed off for yet another assault on Nhpum Ga: "We have been attacking up this g------ hill for four days now and getting two-bitted to death by casualties and getting nowhere. Today, let's take what casualties we have to, to get the job done. In the long run you will lose fewer men. Good luck" (Hunter 1963, pp. 77–78). On April 9, the 3d Battalion broke through and the siege at Nhpum Ga was finished. There was no further enemy activity on April 10 and 11. Merrill wrote later: "At Nhpum Ga the best part of 3 Jap Bns were engaged. It was a Jap defeat as they withdrew all the way to Myitkyina" (quoted in McGee 1987, p. 135). The Japanese fierce counterattack simply disappeared as Tanaka began to focus his concerns on holding Myitkyina; he did not want to disperse his troop assets in the hills above Kamaing. Galahad had lost 59 killed and 379 men were evacuated (including Merrill with another heart attack) with wounds or sickness. Tanaka lost at least 400 irreplaceable men as his casualties defending the Kamaing Road in the Mogaung Valley and counterattacking the 2d and 3d Marauder battalions began to seriously mount up. The 18th Division's ad hoc assaulting force failed to push back the Americans and seize Nhpum Ga, leaving a sizable threat on Tanaka's right flank. As a result of the defeat, the remaining elements of the Japanese 3/114th Infantry Regiment returned to Myitkyina intact but badly battered.

Technical Sergeant Chester Degrange, 3d Battalion, cleans the firing tube of his 60mm mortar after inspection was ordered as a morale booster by Colonel Hunter following the lifting of the siege at Nhpum Ga, on April 9, 1944. Both the 60mm and 81mm mortars were vital and effective weapons for the Marauders in the jungle since they lacked their own artillery. (NARA 111-SC-277390)

Despite the victory at Nhpum Ga, "the fighting edge of the most mobile and most obedient force that Stilwell had was worn dull" (Romanus and Sunderland 1970, p. 191). After fighting over 500 miles of jungle, the Marauders were exhausted having survived on a diet of cold K-rations inadequate to maintain strength and succumbing to malaria, dysentery, and scrub typhus. Yet, Stilwell intended to keep his Galahad force in the field, past its promised 90-day limit by their initial organizer, the recently deceased Wingate, for his final thrust to Myitkyina. To Stilwell and his staff, by late April the Japanese 18th Division was under incredible pressure with the Chinese just north of Inkangahtawng and only 20 miles from Kamaing. The Chindit block and "stronghold" just north of Mawlu at "White City," 80 miles south of Myitkyina, had interrupted the single railway into northern Burma, which terminated at Myitkyina, compelling the Japanese to use shipping up the Irrawaddy River as their principal method to supply both Myitkyina and Mogaung. Also, in the Irrawaddy Valley, British-led Kachin and Gurkha forces had already captured the 2/114th Infantry Regiment's forward base at Sumprabum and were now threatening another Japanese supply base at Nsopzup, just 45 miles north of Myitkina. Despite these advances against the enemy, Hunter, the consummate professional, had to put his staff to work planning a move for his exhausted Marauders to Myitkyina, and deployed Kachin scouts over the Kumon Range to find a concealed route to attack the Japanese hub on the Irrawaddy, 65 miles to the southeast.

THE CAPTURE OF MYITKYINA AIRFIELD

By late April, the Allied offensive in northern Burma was putting heavy but very slow pressure on the Japanese. Stilwell's column had gained 35 miles and was fighting just north of Inkangahtawng, 20 miles from Kamaing. In the Irrawaddy River valley, British-led Gurkha and Kachin levies were moving on Nsopzup, a Japanese supply point on the river between Myitkyina and Sumprabum. Myitkyina, 170 miles to the southeast of the Ledo Road's origin in Assam, was Tanaka's main base of operations for his 18th Division and was garrisoned by elements of Maruyama's 114th Infantry Regiment. Stilwell's quest included the only all-weather airstrip in northern Burma, which had been proven to be the major Japanese fighter base to interdict the ATC transports flying from India to southwest China as well as greatly facilitating resupply and evacuation of wounded. Moreover, Myitkyina lay at the head of the Irradwaddy River's navigable portion. Clearly, occupying Myitkyina afforded control of all of northern Burma.

The advance to Myitkyina across the Kumon Range, April 28–May 17, 1944.

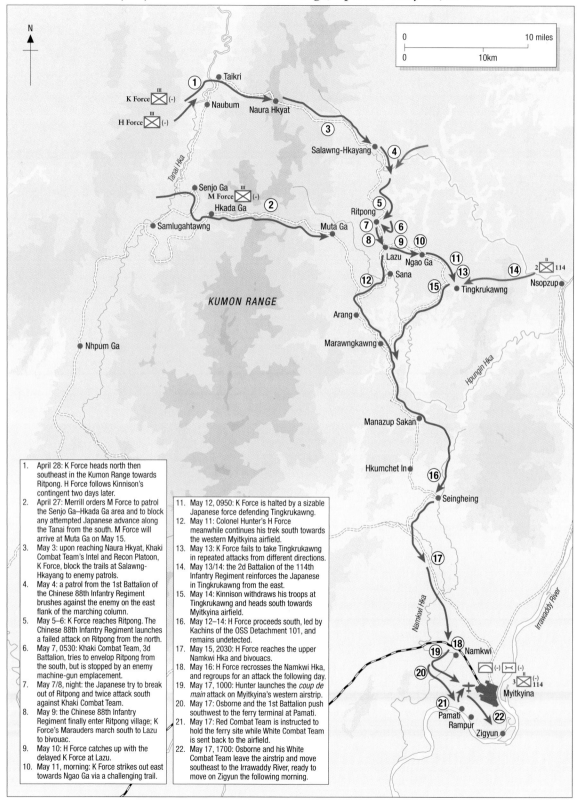

1. April 28: K Force heads north then southeast in the Kumon Range towards Ritpong. H Force follows Kinnison's contingent two days later.
2. April 27: Merrill orders M Force to patrol the Senjo Ga–Hkada Ga area and to block any attempted Japanese advance along the Tanai from the south. M Force will arrive at Muta Ga on May 15.
3. May 3: upon reaching Naura Hkyat, Khaki Combat Team's Intel and Recon Platoon, K Force, block the trails at Salawng-Hkayang to enemy patrols.
4. May 4: a patrol from the 1st Battalion of the Chinese 88th Infantry Regiment brushes against the enemy on the east flank of the marching column.
5. May 5–6: K Force reaches Ritpong. The Chinese 88th Infantry Regiment launches a failed attack on Ritpong from the north.
6. May 7, 0530: Khaki Combat Team, 3d Battalion, tries to envelop Ritpong from the south, but is stopped by an enemy machine-gun emplacement.
7. May 7/8, night: the Japanese try to break out of Ritpong and twice attack south against Khaki Combat Team.
8. May 9: the Chinese 88th Infantry Regiment finally enter Ritpong village; K Force's Marauders march south to Lazu to bivouac.
9. May 10: H Force catches up with the delayed K Force at Lazu.
10. May 11, morning: K Force strikes out east towards Ngao Ga via a challenging trail.
11. May 12, 0950: K Force is halted by a sizable Japanese force defending Tingkrukawng.
12. May 11: Colonel Hunter's H Force meanwhile continues his trek south towards the western Myitkyina airfield.
13. May 13: K Force fails to take Tingkrukawng in repeated attacks from different directions.
14. May 13/14: the 2d Battalion of the 114th Infantry Regiment reinforces the Japanese in Tingkrukawng from the east.
15. May 14: Kinnison withdraws his troops at Tingkrukawng and heads south towards Myitkyina airfield.
16. May 12–14: H Force proceeds south, led by Kachins of the OSS Detachment 101, and remains undetected.
17. May 15, 2030: H Force reaches the upper Namkwi Hka and bivouacs.
18. May 16: H Force recrosses the Namkwi Hka, and regroups for an attack the following day.
19. May 17, 1000: Hunter launches the *coup de main* attack on Myitkyina's western airstrip.
20. May 17: Osborne and the 1st Battalion push southwest to the ferry terminal at Pamati.
21. May 17: Red Combat Team is instructed to hold the ferry site while White Combat Team is sent back to the airfield.
22. May 17, 1700: Osborne and his White Combat Team leave the airstrip and move southeast to the Irrawaddy River, ready to move on Zigyun the following morning.

Taking advantage of the aforementioned developments, Stilwell planned to continue his drive down the Mogaung corridor towards Kamaing, with the Chinese 65th Infantry Regiment protecting the right flank of the 22d Division as before. Stilwell wanted to move down the Mogaung Valley on Kamaing with such strength as to deceive Tanaka that this was the main Sino-American objective. Stilwell hoped that if kept confronted by his Chinese troops, no Japanese reinforcements could be sent to Myitkyina and possibly Tanaka would move troops from the city on the Irrawaddy to defend Kamaing, which was the last stronghold for the Japanese in the Hukawng and Mogaung valleys.

His major plan to capture Myitkyina was called "End Run," using characteristic American football parlance, and for the third time his Marauders were to take part in a wide flanking move to the east of the main effort over the Kumon Range, which formed the eastern boundary of the Mogaung Valley. This was to be the most difficult of the Marauders' missions; they were to strike at Myitkyina itself, the chief objective of the campaign. For Stilwell, given the delays and slowdowns already experienced and several failures to eliminate the 18th Division in battle, with Sun Li-jen and Liao Yao-hsiang deliberately stalling, there was no chance left but a risky, enveloping strike. Boatner commented on the Myitkyina assault: "It was, indeed, a 'desperate gamble' and almost resulted in a disaster" (Boatner 1971, p. 35). As of April 21, Stilwell determined that a rapid, secret penetration across the mountains by a striking force of Galahad and Chinese to seize the Myitkyina airstrip was needed, with reinforcements and heavy weapons to be flown in after its capture to complete the seizure of the town.

For his assaults on Myitkyina, Stilwell had the remnants of his Marauder battalions, although these formations were showing fatigue and sickness from the grueling marches and unfavorable conditions. Since February 9, the Marauders had marched and fought through 500 miles of difficult Burmese terrain. After Nhpum Ga, the troops were exhausted and there remained only 1,400 men out of the original total of 2,997. During most of their 80-day trek, they suffered from malnutrition, leech-induced "Naga sores," amebic dysentery, mite-vectored scrub typhus, malaria, and many other causes of fever. Stilwell was fully cognizant of the drain placed on both the Marauders and Chindits with their ceaseless combat; however, he was consumed by his own driving military ambition to reach Myitkyina. Most of the American troops kept on marching because they believed, as Merrill had indicated to his battalion commanders, "that the capture of Myitkyina was the end of the road: after that, the men would be evacuated" (Allen 2000, p. 365)

The Marauders would have two new Chinese infantry regiments – the 150th and 88th from the 50th and 30th divisions, respectively – attached to them and a screen of Kachin tribesmen, who possessed great jungle skills and animus towards the Japanese, along with the OSS-led Detachment 101 with their Kachin Rangers. The additional Chinese and Kachin troops brought Merrill's strength to about 7,000 men for the Myitkyina operation. Boatner stated: "It was the first joint operation of the Marauders with the Chinese. The Chinese had mostly just arrived from China, had also never operated with Americans and were far inferior to the veteran 22nd and 38th Divisions of the CAI in weapons, experience and combat efficiency" (Boatner 1971, p. 39). Both the 22d and 38th divisions were still in the Mogaung Valley when Stilwell unleashed his *coup de main* against the airfield at Myitkyina.

End Run was not to approach Myitkyina from Mogaung, but to put a force across the hills of the Kumon Range, with the help of the Kachins, and strike at Myitkyina from the north. The Kachins warned that "the steep Kumon Mountain range could not be crossed by pack animals except in dry weather but Stilwell was determined to make the attempt" (Tuchman 1970, pp. 444–45). At one point they had to climb a 6,000ft pass, and upon reaching the summit a cold bitter wind hit them. Hunter had earlier argued, during the retreat to Nhpum Ga, that if Stilwell had kept his forces, firepower, and airpower concentrated to first capture Kamaing, he then would have had his entire force to take Mogaung, some 20 miles south, and then with the railway capture Myitkyina. However, Hunter, the consummate professional officer, called his subordinates together to plan for the strike on Myitkyina's western airfield.

Three combat forces were created by Hunter for the mission. His own one, H Force, was to comprise the Chinese 150th Infantry Regiment, the 1st Battalion of Galahad with its Red and White combat teams, under the command of Osborne, and the 3d Company of the Animal Transport Regiment along with a battery of 75mm pack howitzers of the Chinese 22d Division's artillery. K Force, under Colonel Henry L. Kinnison, was made up of the Chinese 88th Infantry Regiment and Galahad's 3d Battalion led by Beach. M Force, under McGee, had as its nucleus the Marauders' 2d Battalion and 300 Kachins. The losses at Nhpum Ga had wreaked havoc on McGee's combat-team organizational structure. Instead, his roughly 50 percent Marauder contingent was formed into two rifle companies, one heavy weapons and a battalion headquarters company.

K Force left for the Kumon Range on April 28 followed by H Force, which departed on April 30. Merrill had recovered from his cardiac ailment and remained at headquarters at Naubum, which Stilwell had visited the previous day to give final orders for the mission. Stilwell's operational plan for his forces' movements "called for crossing the Kumon Range with H and

Colonel Charles Hunter (right) discusses plans for the attack on the Myitkyina airfield with Major Hodges (left) and Lieutenant-Colonel William H. Combs (center). Combs, a liaison officer with the Chinese, would die a month after the successful capture of the airfield while trying to warn a green American unit of a Japanese ambush. (USAMHI)

SWORD ATTACK ON MARAUDERS OF 1ST BATTALION, MAY 17, 1944 (PP. 68–69)

On the morning of May 17, 1944, Osborne took his 1st Battalion from their bivouac at Namkwi and headed southwest towards Pamati on the Irrawaddy River, as elements of the Chinese 150th Infantry Regiment headed to capture the main airfield west of the town of Myitkyina in Stilwell's *coup de main.*

By taking the ferry terminal at Pamati, the 1st Battalion would control the nearest crossing of the Irrawaddy River in proximity to the airstrip. Evidently, there were Japanese troops around Pamati, for a sniper kept firing at them. Leaving a platoon to hold the village, the battalion took the road that led directly back to the airstrip. The village of Pamati stood in the midst of a flat area surrounded by rice paddies. Further off from the village, about 400–500yd, the ground rose and was covered with a dense growth of scrub and vines. On the way, some natives ran up to a platoon of Osborne's Marauders and informed them that 30 Japanese were blocking the road up ahead from well dug-in positions around the base of a large tree. These were elements of the 114th Infantry Regiment of the 18th Division.

A trio of Marauders (1) dropped their packs and in single file walked slowly through the dense scrub to reconnoiter. At this point a sword-wielding Japanese lieutenant with a pistol (2) leaped out of a concealed foxhole to attack the lead Marauder armed with an M1 Garand rifle with attached bayonet, not more than 7–10yd away. Other Japanese infantrymen exited the foxhole behind the lieutenant.

The foxhole (3) was the simplest form of defensive position and the Japanese were adept at constructing them in unlikely and, thus, unexpected places. More permanent sites were often lined with wooden planks or concrete, but much the same degree of protection from small arms and mortar fire was obtained by the use of earth and logs. Often such foxholes would have underground passages from which Japanese soldiers would emerge when the ground had been overrun to attack the Americans and Chinese from the rear. Somewhat disconcertingly for their opponents, the exits from these submerged foxholes were so well camouflaged and concealed that they were not easily detected. Allied troops often only detected Japanese positions when they came under fire at close range or when hidden infantry exited from their prepared positions to attack isolated or small groups of the enemy, as here. Some of these foxholes would be covered with vegetation transplanted with such skill that it was still growing; while in more barren areas rocks and stones would have been so arranged that the eye would be led away from the vital area and so fail to detect it.

Japanese tactical defense was based on heavy machine guns, which were protected by light machine guns, rifle pits, and infantry concealed in foxholes. An attack on one position would draw fire from two or more mutually supporting positions. Often the Japanese would hold their fire until the enemy had closed to within 10yd. The Japanese often had no intention of escaping at this stage of the Myitkyina campaign, and they became known for their tenacity and willingness to engage in hand-to-hand combat using bayonets, swords, knives, or bare hands.

K Forces via the Naura Hkyet (a 6,100-foot pass), then turning south on Ritpong. From there the two forces would take separate routes that would later converge on Myitkyina. M Force would be in position to cover the south flank, the most likely danger spot" (Romanus and Sunderland 1970, p. 223). M Force started its trek on May 7. The monsoon season was about to begin, which would make the trek and air resupply even more treacherous.

On May 5, Kinnison enveloped Ritpong and it took until May 9 for Ritpong's Japanese defenders, believed to be in considerable strength, to fall to the Chinese 88th Infantry Regiment's troops attacking from the north while Marauder combat teams hacked out a jungle trail to the south of the village to set up a blocking ambush position. In the meantime, H Force overtook and passed through K Force on May 10 at Lazu, about 35 miles northwest of Myitkyina, on its southward march to the airfield. On May 12, K Force feigned an attack on Nsopzup on the Irrawaddy well north of Myitkyina, which was being attacked by British-led Kachin and Gurkha natives. Later that day, Kinnison's troops clashed with the Japanese, comprising a reinforced battalion in well dug-in machine-gun positions, at Tingkrukawng. On May 13, the Marauders and Chinese were still unable to overtake the Japanese, who were now receiving considerable reinforcements from the east, so Kinnison was ordered by Merrill to disengage and pick up Hunter's trail and follow it to Myitkyina. K Force had provided sufficient diversionary activity to enable Hunter's force to continue its southwardly trek towards Myitkyina. Unfortunately, Kinnison contracted scrub typhus and subsequently died during his evacuation.

By the beginning of May, Stilwell submitted his updated plans to the chiefs of staff. First was the capture of both the Mogaung and Myitkyina areas. Second was to build airfields that could be used even throughout the monsoon season. Third was the reiteration of his statement to open the road from Myitkyina to Kunming, thereby re-establishing the Burma Road. To accomplish this, Stilwell had two additional Chinese divisions, the 14th and 50th, giving him a total of five of Chiang's divisions and the remnants of the Marauders and Chindits as well as Kachin irregulars.

General Sun Li-jen (left), commanding Chinese 38th Division, with Colonel Henry Kinnison (center), the K Force commander for the Myitkyina assault, and Brigadier Merrill (right), discusses the upcoming plans to attack Myitkyina, at Naubum in late April 1944. Kinnison later contracted scrub typhus on the march over the Kumon Range to the airfield, and died. (NARA 559282 MM 220)

After the *coup de main* capture of the western airfield at Myitkyina on May 17, Stilwell (center, with carbine slung over right shoulder) confers with Merrill (second from left) and the Myitkyina attack force leader Hunter (back to camera), as US Signal Corps photographers record the meeting. An L-5 Sentinel liaison aircraft, which shuttled Stilwell to different battlefield sites, is in the background. (USAMHI)

While K Force was engaging the Japanese at Tingkrukawng on May 12–13, Hunter pushed his Sino-American force southwards on a jungle trail first along the Hpungin Hka and then the Namkwi Hka, until he arrived to just south of Namkwi on the Mogaung–Myitkyina railroad, which was about "two miles from the principal Myitkyina airstrip that lay almost due west of Myitkyina itself" (Romanus and Sunderland 1970, p. 226) without being seen by the Japanese or any Burmese natives. With H Force's arrival on the railway on the night of May 15/16, it appeared that total surprise was achieved and Hunter's reconnaissance troops estimated that there were only 100 Japanese and Burmese laborers at the airfield. Also, Hunter was aware that the Japanese habitually withdrew from the airfield during daylight into the distant thick scrub to avoid Allied bombing and strafing. At 1000hrs on May 17, Hunter sent in the Chinese 150th Infantry Regiment of the 50th Division, which captured the Myitkyina airstrip within 45 minutes. The Galahad component of H Force, Red Combat Team, took the ferry terminal on the Irrawaddy at Pamati at 1100hrs, immediately due southwest of the airfield, thereby gaining control of the nearest crossing of the wide river. At 1700hrs, Osborne and White Combat Team of H Force left the now-captured airstrip and moved southeast to the river to take up positions near the village of Rampur. Another village and ferry at Zigyun, also on the river, would be attacked in the morning. However, the second airstrip north of the town of Myitkyina was not attacked on that day.

At 1050hrs on May 17, Stilwell received the prearranged signal – "In the Ring" – from Merrill, indicating that the airfield was reached. Hunter wanted to make sure his perimeter at the airfield was secure and at 1530hrs sent a request for airlifted reinforcements. On Old's orders, the C-47 transports with guns and ammunition started on their way to Myitkyina airfield within minutes of Hunter's communication. One of Stilwell's diary entries for this day read, "WILL THIS BURN UP THE LIMIES" (Stilwell 1991, p. 296). Even Churchill questioned Mountbatten as to how "the Americans by a brilliant feat of arms have landed us in Myitkyina" (Churchill 1951, p. 570). Mountbatten, in his communiqué to Stilwell and his troops, declared it "a feat which will live in military history," but did not fail to mention the Chindits, "who have been severing Japanese communications between Myitkyina and the south" (quoted in Tuchman 1970, pp. 448–49) for a share of the credit.

As no Japanese counterattack ensued at the airfield on May 17, Hunter questioned whether he or the enemy could build up strength more speedily. He called for K and M forces to urgently march to the airfield. Also, one

An American airborne engineer of an antiaircraft artillery company mans a .50-cal. machine gun, while a fellow soldier readies another box magazine of ammunition, at the Myitkyina airstrip. A C-47 Dakota transport sits idle on the runway behind them. (USAMHI).

battalion of the Chinese 89th Infantry Regiment arrived by air, in transports and gliders, from Ledo late on the afternoon of May 17. Hunter was still of the belief that the Japanese did not hold Myitkyina in strength and he decided to extend his seizure of the airfield with a surprise assault on the town itself. However, American commanders in the rear, notably Stratemeyer (FEAF commander), wanted to reinforce the airstrip rather than commit more men, mules, and ammunition to the assault on Myitkina town. Thus, in addition to the Chinese 2/88th Infantry Regiment, only a company of the 879th Engineer Aviation Battalion along with a battery of .50-cal. antiaircraft machine guns came in via glider as bad weather closed in on the Myitkyina airfield late on May 17. Thus, by intervening, Stratemeyer had "upset the planned schedule of resupply and reinforcement by ordering the W and X Troops of the 69th Light (Anti-aircraft) Regiment, a British unit, to be flown in" (Romanus and Sunderland 1970, p. 228) on May 18. Both Hunter and Merrill were dismayed as they would now be left with a relatively weak Allied offensive force, devoid of the infantry and supplies that were needed for an effective assault against Myitkyina town immediately after the airstrip's seizure. Although Stratemeyer's move could be understood on the precautionary grounds of properly defending the newly acquired airstrip from an enemy air attack, this would become one of the reasons for the campaign transforming into a siege for 78 days rather than another *coup de main* to capture Myitkyina town.

A British crew on alert at their 40mm Bofors gun on July 18, 1944 at the Myitkyina airfield. Japanese air attacks occurred frequently in an attempt to slow the arrival of reinforcements and supplies for the Allied airhead established on May 17. A fighter can just be seen taking off at far left. (NARA 111-SC-262536)

77TH BRIGADE AT MOGAUNG

A few days after Wingate's death in a plane crash on March 24, 1944, Major-General Walter "Joe" Lentaigne assumed command of the Chindits. Under the latter's leadership, the Chindit LRP concept was abandoned and Wingate's guidelines on "strongholds" radically altered. Also, Lentaigne, under Stilwell's direction, was blamed for ordering Calvert's 77th Indian Infantry Brigade to cover Stilwell's left flank, although, it was understood, that one of the major tasks assigned to the Chindits for Operation Thursday was to assist Stilwell's Sino-American forces to take Mogaung and Myitkyina by disrupting 18th Division's lines of communication in the Hukawng and Mogaung valleys. Unfortunately for 77th Indian Infantry Brigade, the majority of Chindit casualties would occur after Lentaigne changed the scope of the LRP mission to that of a conventional infantry one to take Mogaung.

After marching over the Kumon Range, on May 17 Stilwell's Sino-American force captured the Myitkyina airfield, west of the town, in a *coup de main*. From a strategic standpoint, Stilwell no longer wanted the Chindits to attract the enemy's attention away from his men, but rather, while still blocking the railway, to focus the Chindit main effort against the town of Mogaung, which threatened Stilwell's lines of communication to the west of the Myitkyina airfield and represented a perpetual enemy force in the Sino-American rear. With the continued Chinese advance down the Kamaing Road, 18th Division was also in grave danger, especially if Mogaung was to be captured by the Allies. On May 29, Calvert signaled his desire to Lentaigne to remain in his position in the Gangaw Range opposite the new Chindit stronghold of "Blackpool" (after his brigade had already withdrawn from both the "White City" and "Broadway" strongholds), and resume guerrilla or LRP methods to harass the Japanese. As previously noted, Calvert was reluctant to become conventional infantry for Stilwell. Lentaigne responded by instructing him to take Mogaung with 77th Brigade. In order to secure Mogaung, Calvert wanted to have a "secure base" that could be easily defended from a Japanese counterattack, which would also have built within it a light plane airstrip, a drop zone for supplies, a hospital and ammunition dumps. Since he would not have conventional artillery, he would have to rely upon 3in. mortars. His brigade was to use approximately 60,000 mortar bombs in the capture of Mogaung. Even so, everything would depend on air support, since this would constitute Calvert's response to the firepower of the 18th Division's artillery in Mogaung. In order to direct air strikes properly, Calvert would need to secure high ground, offering both improved visibility and longer radio-transmission ranges, from which his RAF liaison officers could control the sorties and make adjustments.

Mogaung was surrounded by the Wettauk and Namyin *chaungs* to the southeast and west, respectively, and to the north by the wide and swift-flowing (6 knots) Mogaung River, which flowed in an easterly semicircular direction from the town to the Tapaw Ferry and then to the Irrawaddy River. The Wettauk Chaung had a steel-girder road bridge that crossed it at the village of Pinhmi. The Mogaung River just north of the town was bridged by a damaged steel-girder railroad bridge on the Myitkyina–Rangoon railroad. Lakum village was in the hills to the south overlooking the Pinhmi Bridge and this was from where Calvert planned his attack against the steel structure over the Wettauk Chaung to reach the eastern edge of the town of Mogaung. Loilaw village was where the railway from Myitkyina to Rangoon crossed the Namyin Chaung, about four miles south of Mogaung. Mahaung and Naungkaiktaw villages were on the west side of the Wettauk Chaung south of the Pinhmi Bridge, and were to be the initial objectives of the 3/6th Gurkha Rifles and 1st South Staffordshires, attacking across a ford discovered on June 9, after the two 1st Lancashire Fusiliers platoons' unsuccessful attempt to storm the Pinhmi Bridge on June 8. Other objectives for the 3/6th Gurkhas and 1st South Staffordshires were the Court House and railway station in Mogaung itself.

At Mogaung, the original Chindit organization – two columns, each acting independently, formed out of one battalion in order to conduct guerrilla warfare efficiently – would now be reversed, and two columns were merged into one battalion. Even after Stilwell's capture of Myitkyina airfield on May 17, it was possible for the Japanese to move in and out of Myitkyina town, in spite of the American and Chinese "encirclement." Leading Japanese elements of 3/128th Infantry and Headquarters 128th Infantry (53d Division) began to arrive at Mogaung from Myitkyina during the early days of June 1944 to strengthen Mogaung's eastern defences and fend off the Chindit descent on that town, after the last Chindit stronghold of "Blackpool" was evacuated. With other elements of the 3/114th Infantry, Tanaka's divisional artillery, an ad hoc composite force of field hospital and service unit troops, Mogaung was strongly garrisoned. In fact, the Japanese had roughly 3,500 men at Mogaung. Calvert's 77th Indian Infantry Brigade would therefore encounter a Japanese garrison at Mogaung that was both entrenched and reinforced. A direct frontal assault was immediately eliminated as a possibility by the Chindits, whose ranks had been thinned by combat casualties and disease since their glider airlanding at "Broadway" on March 5.

Calvert had decided that his brigade should advance during a battle of attrition against successive Japanese outposts and occupied villages along a narrow east–west line. The brigadier had reasoned that rather than attacking Mogaung directly from the south from the village of Loilaw, the direction from which the Japanese would expect his assault to come from, he would confuse the enemy by putting in an initial attack from the southeast, through flooded marshes and lakes and, ultimately, get across Pinhmi Bridge to the eastern side of Mogaung. The Japanese positions were to be reconnoitered, then "aerial artillery" – usually delivered by P-51 Mustangs of the 1st Air Commando Group – would be brought to bear on the defenders. This in turn would be followed up by infantry, assaulting behind a mortar barrage and direct Vickers machine-gun fire, utilizing grenades and flamethrowers. Some Japanese strongpoints were dug in beneath Burmese houses, and for these the flamethrowers would be used since the loopholes of these entrenchments were covered with metal grilles to deflect grenades.

Chindits from Calvert's 77th Indian Infantry Brigade fire their 3in. mortar to reduce Japanese positions in heavily fortified Mogaung in June 1944. The Chindit in the background is spotting where rounds land. After Wingate's death, many Chindits, especially Calvert, were dismayed by Stilwell's insistence on using them as conventional infantry rather than LRP specialists in the capture of Mogaung. (USAMHI)

1. June 2: the Lancashire Fusiliers and the South Staffords attack Mogaung from the southeast, along a range of hills, and capture the sizable village of Lakum with substantial ammunition dumps, a hospital and several headquarters units. The Chindits begin to receive regular supply drops and build an airstrip for L-5 Sentinel aircraft to evacuate wounded.

2. Early June: leading elements of the Japanese II/128th and I/151st Infantry regiments, 53d Division, began to arrive from Myitkyina to strengthen Mogaung's eastern defenses.

3. June 3: the Lancashire Fusiliers seize Loihinche and establish 77th Indian Infantry Brigade's headquarters there; Calvert reconnoiters the town of Mogaung.

4. June 3: two commando platoons of the Lancashire Fusiliers, under Captain George Butler, are stationed to the rear of 77th Indian Infantry Brigade at Tapaw Ferry on the Mogaung River to secure a potential Chindit escape route to the east.

5. June 3: the III/6th Gurkhas capture the village between Lakum and Pinhmi to build a light L-5 Sentinel liaison aircraft strip; they call it "Gurkha Village."

6. June 8, early: the South Staffords destroy Japanese ammunition dumps at Pinhmi, which are defended by elements of the III/128th Infantry Regiment, 53d Division. The Lancashire Fusiliers pass through the village on their way down to the bridge over the Wettauk Chaung.

7. June 8, midday: a platoon tries to work its way along a ditch towards the bridge, but find it too overgrown and the water too deep to bring effective fire on the Japanese positions on the far side of the bridge. A few of the fusiliers manage to get onto the bridge itself.

8. June 8, 1800hrs: not having completed a proper reconnaissance, Calvert meets with the Fusiliers' commanding officer, Major David Monteith, at Pinhmi Bridge. After laying a mortar barrage onto the bridge's span and along the far side of the Wettauk Chaung, Calvert orders two Fusilier platoons to rush across the span, unaware of the entrenched machine-gun positions and rifle pits of the III/114th Japanese Infantry. The attack fails within minutes, incurring heavy casualties.

9. June 9, dawn: after fording the Wettauk Chaung south of the Pinhmi Bridge, Calvert attacks along a flooded path through the marsh with the South Staffords and the Gurkhas, surprising the Japanese holding Mahaung and capturing it. A South Staffords company, under the command of Major "Nip" Hilton, encounters Japanese infantry in a bamboo clump near Ywathitgale, a Japanese administrative headquarters, and after repeated enemy counterattacks the Chindits finally drive them off. Major Ron Degg, with the rest of his 1st South Staffordshire Battalion, clears Ywathitgale village and reaches the Pinhmi–Mogaung road to the west of the bridge still controlled by the enemy.

TO RANGOON

10. June 9, midday: leaving one Gurkha company at Mahaung, Calvert orders the South Staffords to attack the Japanese in the rear on the Pinhmi Bridge while the Gurkhas move up from the front; however, the Gurkha attack is delayed until the following day.

11. June 10, 0700hrs: the Gurkhas set upon the bunkered-in enemy from behind with rifle fire and grenades, but the attack is repelled and the Gurkhas are forced to retreat into the jungle. By 0900hrs, the Gurkhas, advancing on the Japanese position from the downstream flank through the waist-deep mud and dense reeds of the Wettauk Chaung, finally start to silence some of the Japanese positions. At midday, 77th Indian Infantry Brigade is securely established along the axis of the Pinhmi–Mogaung road with two battalions up and one in the Pinhmi Bridge area. Chindit casualties in the encirclement and capture of the Pinhmi Bridge are in the region of 130 killed and wounded.

12. June 11, 1200hrs: the court house is captured by 77th Indian Infantry Brigade, and the area extending to the Mogaung River and to the outskirts of Natyigon is cleared of Japanese.

13. June 12, evening: the remainder of the Japanese II/128th and I/151st Infantry regiments, 53d Division, arrive from Myitkyina to strengthen Mogaung's eastern defenses.

14. June 16–18: the Chinese 114th Infantry Regiment under Colonel Li arrives at Gurkhaywa, just north of the Mogaung River. Mogaung can now be sealed off against further Japanese reinforcement and the Chinese field guns can reply to the Japanese artillery sited to the west of the town.

15. June 24: the South Staffords and Gurkhas are ordered to take the last outer bastion, Natyigon.

16. June 24: elements of the Chinese 114th Infantry Regiment fail to roll up the Japanese last line of defense dug in along the railroad embankment. The Chindits are forced to halt along this line.

17. June 26, morning: both Chinese and Gurkhas advance into Mogaung without drawing any fire 16 days after capturing Pinhmi Bridge. Those Japanese who are still fit make oil-drum rafts in the hope of drifting downriver to Myitkyina, still held by the Japanese.

THE CAPTURE OF MOGAUNG BY CALVERT'S CHINDITS, JUNE 2–26, 1944

The villages of Mahaung and Naungkaiktaw were the initial objectives of the Gurkhas and South Staffordshire battalions attacking across a ford discovered on June 9 after the failed assault of two platoons of the Lancashire Fusiliers to storm the bridge on June 8. Pinhmi Bridge would not be captured until June 10 in an attack by the Gurkhas that commenced from behind the Wettauk Chaung's western embankment. Other objectives for these battalions were Mogaung's court house and railroad station. From these sites, the Chindits, and eventually the late-arriving Chinese, would assault Natyigon, the Japanese outer bastion, and then Mogaung proper. This battle of attrition would last until June 26, 1944. Mogaung's capture would finally protect Stilwell's left flank at the airstrip to the west of Myitkyina town.

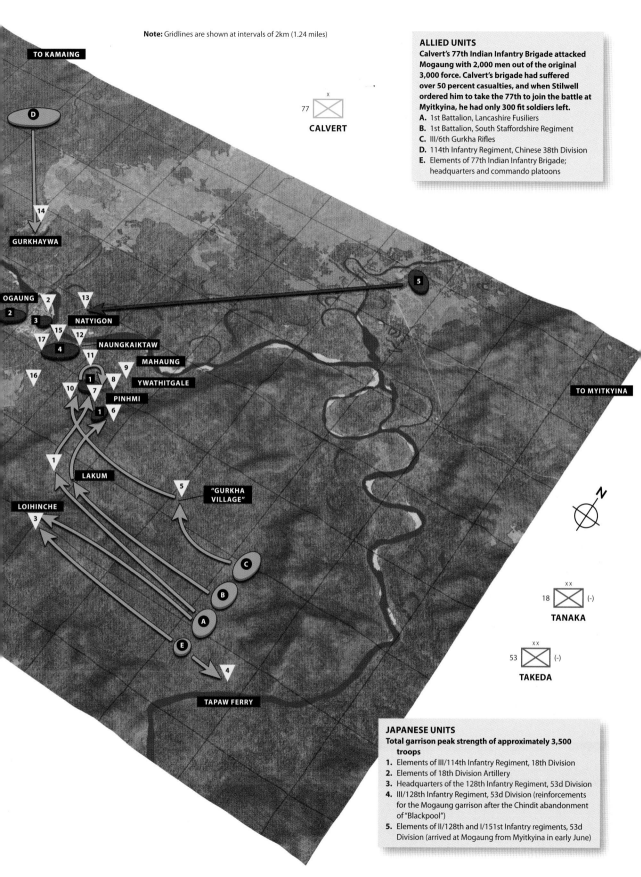

Note: Gridlines are shown at intervals of 2km (1.24 miles)

TO KAMAING

GURKHAYWA

OGAUNG

NATYIGON

NAUNGKAIKTAW

MAHAUNG

YWATHITGALE

PINHMI

LAKUM

"GURKHA VILLAGE"

LOIHINCHE

TAPAW FERRY

TO MYITKYINA

77
CALVERT

18 (-)
TANAKA

53 (-)
TAKEDA

ALLIED UNITS
Calvert's 77th Indian Infantry Brigade attacked
Mogaung with 2,000 men out of the original
3,000 force. Calvert's brigade had suffered
over 50 percent casualties, and when Stilwell
ordered him to take the 77th to join the battle at
Myitkyina, he had only 300 fit soldiers left.
A. 1st Battalion, Lancashire Fusiliers
B. 1st Battalion, South Staffordshire Regiment
C. III/6th Gurkha Rifles
D. 114th Infantry Regiment, Chinese 38th Division
E. Elements of 77th Indian Infantry Brigade;
   headquarters and commando platoons

JAPANESE UNITS
Total garrison peak strength of approximately 3,500
troops
1. Elements of III/114th Infantry Regiment, 18th Division
2. Elements of 18th Division Artillery
3. Headquarters of the 128th Infantry Regiment, 53d Division
4. III/128th Infantry Regiment, 53d Division (reinforcements
   for the Mogaung garrison after the Chindit abandonment
   of "Blackpool")
5. Elements of II/128th and I/151st Infantry regiments, 53d
   Division (arrived at Mogaung from Myitkyina in early June)

Calvert had replied to Lentaigne that he would use June 6 as his day for the main attack on Mogaung; however, the difficulties of the terrain and the tenacity of the Japanese in their outposts would retard his "timings" until the third week of June. The 77th Indian Infantry Brigade tactical assault began on June 2 as his Chindit force advanced from the southeast across two miles of open country studded with villages, each one fortified with bunkers dug underneath their huts, creating interlocking fields of fire. A village captured in this fashion would then serve as the takeoff point for the next fortified village to be assaulted. On June 2, the 1st Lancashire Fusiliers and 1st South Staffordshires, moving along a range of hills to the east of Mogaung, were ordered to attack and capture the sizable village of Lakum, where there were substantial ammunition dumps, a hospital and several Japanese headquarter units. Once established in Lakum, the Chindits built an airstrip to accommodate L-5 aircraft to bring in supplies and evacuate wounded infantrymen. The next day, Loihinche fell to the Chindits and Calvert established 77th Indian Infantry Brigade headquarters there. Elsewhere that day, two commando platoons from the 1st Lancashire Fusiliers captured Tapaw Ferry on the Mogaung River, should Calvert need to retreat eastwards, while the 3/6th Gurkhas seized a nearby settlement, renamed it "Gurkha Village," and built another liaison aircraft airstrip there.

From Lakum, Pinhmi, where a steel road bridge took the Tapaw Ferry–Mogaung Road over the 30yd-wide flooded and unfordable Wettauk Chaung to the east of Mogaung, was seen as the next step forward. The Japanese were in excellent concealed positions high up on the 15ft embankment leading to the far side of the bridge. Early on the morning of June 8, the 1st South Staffordshires destroyed Japanese ammunition dumps in the vicinity of Pinhmi village, which was defended by Japanese infantry from the 3/128th (53d Division), on their way down to the bridge over the Wettauk Chaung. The Japanese defenders at Pinhmi Bridge were a mixed lot. Some had been in Burma since 1942 and had become sick and debilitated from malnutrition and disease. Fresher troops from the IJA 53d Division had recently reinforced them. There, the 1st South Staffordshires halted to let the 1st Lancashire Fusiliers capture Pinhmi village later that day. On the Lancashire Fusiliers' side of the bridge, the road from the village was raised several feet above ground level, with a ditch about 4ft deep choked with grass and bushes on the near side and, on the far side, dense jungle that led to the Mogaung River. Without proper reconnaissance, Calvert ordered two platoons of the 1st Lancashire Fusiliers, under the command of Major David Monteith, to attack across the bridge at 1800hrs on June 8, under cover of a mortar barrage. The mortar rounds failed to dislodge any Japanese defenders from the far embankment, and the Chindit infantrymen were unsure whether there were any Japanese waiting for them in camouflaged fortifications. The two platoons fixed bayonets, climbed out of the ditch and rushed across the bridge. The Japanese on the

A Japanese soldier of the 114th Infantry Regiment, 18th Division, to whom Tanaka had assigned the defense of Myitkyina under Colonel Maruyama Fusayasu. Although the Japanese at Myitkyina numbered over 4,000 men, most were malnourished and disease ridden. (USAMHI)

river's far side waited until the lead fusiliers were halfway across the bridge before firing and, with the Chindits out in the open, many began to fall; chaos ensued as a few of the fusiliers crawled on their bellies along the bridge's surface, trying to push far enough forward to throw hand grenades into the enemy pillboxes, but the Japanese fire was too heavy. At 1815hrs, Monteith ordered a withdrawal. Later that night, the rain ceased and the flooded waters receded somewhat, enabling one of Calvert's patrols to find a ford over the Wettauk Chaung south of the bridge. As dawn broke on June 9, Calvert attacked with the 3/6th Gurkhas and the 1st South Staffordshires; the former led the way across the Wettauk Chaung and along a flooded path through the marsh. The Gurkhas surprised the Japanese platoon from the 3/114th Infantry Regiment holding Mahaung and captured the village. A company of the 1st South Staffordshires, led by Major Hilton, encountered another group of Japanese infantrymen near Ywathitgale, and after a sharp firefight, with repeated counterattacks by the enemy, killed most of them, and drove off the rest. At 1000hrs on June 10, the Gurkhas on their second attempt reduced the Japanese fortifications on the Wettauk Chaung's embankment from behind and, after incurring considerable casualties, took the bridge.

Calvert's brigade was now securely established along the axis of the Pinhmi–Mogaung road, with two battalions up and a third in the Pinhmi Bridge area. Chindit casualties in the encirclement and capture of the bridge were roughly 130 killed and wounded. A larger price was the delay in capturing the bridge, which had given Lieutenant-General Takeda Kaoru time to bring his remaining elements of 2/128th Infantry and 1/151st Infantry (53d Division) into Mogaung to strengthen its eastern and southern perimeter, respectively. By June 12, four battalions of the 53d Division would be facing Calvert, who was still awaiting his Chinese reinforcements, intended to assist him in the assault on Mogaung.

A Caterpillar bulldozer tractor extricates a 2½-ton truck with a Chinese 105mm howitzer in tow. Chinese artillery was necessary for the advance down the Mogaung Valley since Tanaka had employed the guns of his 18th Mountain Artillery Regiment south of the Jambu Bum, which separates the Hukawng Valley from the Mogaung. (USAMHI)

On June 11, the Lancashire Fusiliers fought the Japanese in an area called the Courthouse Triangle, while the South Staffords were sent in to clear the area between the Mogaung River and road, in order to protect 77th Indian Infantry Brigade's right flank. Major Archie Wavell, the son of the field marshal and now India's viceroy, had joined the South Staffords as a replacement officer and was shot in the wrist by a Japanese sniper during this combat and eventually had the hand amputated. On June 12, the 3/6th Gurkhas took over the assault, since the South Stafford companies had been under heavy pressure, and advanced to the Mogaung River within half a mile of the railway bridge; Calvert, however, had only 550 effective men left out of the brigade, many of them suffering from malaria, minor wounds, or trench foot.

The survivors of the brigade were under daily Japanese artillery shelling from the village of Naungkaiktaw to their left flank. At dawn on June 18, Calvert's troops, two companies in strength with flamethrowers, assaulted this Japanese position under cover of the well-patented, intense mortar barrage. By the end of the morning, the village had been cleared with about 50 Japanese killed in the fighting, the rest retreating into Mogaung.

To Calvert's relief, Stilwell's Chinese troops of the 1/114th Infantry Regiment (38th Division) arrived at 1700hrs on June 18, along with artillery, which they used on the Japanese over the next four days. Now Mogaung could be effectively surrounded, with the Chinese to the south, to prevent any further Japanese troops entering the town to reinforce the enemy garrison. Calvert next planned to attack in the direction of Natyigon in the early hours of June 23, after scores of fighter-bomber sorties were flown against the Japanese in Mogaung. Despite the aerial bombardment, concealed Japanese machine guns exacted a high toll on the 500 attacking Chindits: 60 dead and 100 wounded. During the combat at Natyigon that day, in the final attack on the railway bridge, "Captain Allmand, although suffering from trenchfoot, which made it difficult to walk, moved forward along through deep mud and shell-holes and charged a Japanese machine-gun nest single-handed, but he was mortally wounded and died shortly afterwards" (quoted in Chinnery 1997, p. 218). For his heroism, Allmand was awarded a posthumous Victoria Cross. On June 24,

A Japanese soldier lies dead next to his *hinomaru yosegaki* or "flag of the rising sun." These flags featured inscriptions, inscribed by his family, friends, or fellow soldiers, such as poems, good luck phrases, and encouragements, in order to serve as amulets to stop enemy bullets, so soldiers kept them close at hand. To keep true to the warrior or bushido code, not many prisoners were taken in northern Burma. (USAMHI)

after being shelled by the Japanese the previous night, the remaining Lancashire Fusiliers and the Chinese finally captured the railway station's red brick building in Mogaung. It would not be until the next day, 19 days later than his initial "timings" to Lentaigne, that Calvert and his surviving men moved forward again to discover that the Japanese, using a final artillery barrage, had evacuated Mogaung. The costly 24-day campaign would yield Mogaung as the first Burmese town to be retaken. Stilwell's rear at the Myitkyina airfield was now secure from a Japanese attack from Mogaung.

Calvert's brigade had attacked Mogaung with a strength of 2,000 men, regrouped into three battalions, out of the original 3,000 Chindits. By the time the Japanese had finally been driven out of Mogaung, 77th Indian Infantry Brigade had suffered over 50 percent casualties; when Stilwell ordered him to take his surviving Chindits to join the battle at Myitkyina, he had only 300 fit soldiers out of the original 3,000. Ultimately, the Chindits' potential as an LRP force was squandered at Mogaung, essentially fighting hut-to-hut and bunker-to-bunker, first in the numerous surrounding villages and then in the town itself. To add insult to injury, Calvert heard on the BBC on the evening of June 24 that the Americans and Chinese had captured Mogaung. His message to Special Force headquarters, copied to Stilwell, stated: "Americans have captured Mogaung, 77th Brigade is proceeding to take Umbrage" (quoted in Thompson 2003, p. 263).

THE BATTLE AND SIEGE OF MYITKYINA

The town of Myitkyina was still in Japanese hands – and would remain so until the beginning of August – due to a variety of combat and logistical problems at all different levels of command. On May 18, Merrill returned to front-line duty and reorganized the units at Myitkyina airfield as Hunter remained the Marauders' ground force commander. However, after another heart attack, Merrill was evacuated the next day. In the town of Myitkyina, Maruyama Fusayasu, the local Japanese commander, had two understrength battalions of the 114th Infantry Regiment, and with other ancillary units there were perhaps a total of 700 IJA troops. However, the Japanese were reinforcing the town more quickly than Stilwell's Chinese and Americans could attack in force. As a result of the delay in an attack on the town, Major-General Mizukami Genzo of the Japanese 56th Division was able to quickly reinforce Myitkyina. Ultimately, this enabled the Japanese to establish a battle that was more akin to trench warfare than one of maneuver. At peak time during the

A Chinese soldier in former Japanese entrenchments. His weapon, the M1928, had a limited range (394ft) but could produce a cyclic rate of fire of 700 rounds per minute using the .45-cal. bullet with incredible "stopping power." (USAMHI)

battle, the Japanese forces totaled about 4,600 men, but American intelligence estimated that only a quarter of this number was defending Myitkyina town. Another explanation for the failure to take the town of Myitkyina in a timely fashion was that Stilwell's initial combat plans focused obsessively on the airstrip and failed to include a well-coordinated subsequent attack on the town after May 17.

Late on May 17, Hunter was ordered to attack Myitkyina the next day with two battalions of H Force's Chinese 150th Infantry Regiment, while the recently arrived battalion of the 89th Infantry Regiment from Ledo

would defend the airstrip. On May 18, "the rest of the 89th Regiment and a company of heavy mortars were flown in. They were followed next day by the 3/42nd of the Chinese 14th Division. Stilwell arrived to watch operations" (Romanus and Sunderland 1970, p. 230). The Chinese infantry attacked Myitkyina from the north and reached and seized the railroad station. However, after combat that may have involved "friendly fire," the Chinese retreated about a half-mile to the west of the town where they dug in. After Stilwell had visited the airfield and ordered him to attack Myitkyina town, Hunter noted:

A C-47 Dakota transport takes off from the runway at the Myitkyina airfield near a 6ft-deep bomb crater. During the siege of Myitkyina, fighters at the airfield would fly as many as six missions a day to support the ground troops or defend the strip from enemy aircraft attack. (NARA 111-SC-263345)

No commander likes to launch an attack that has little chance of being successful. Such a prospect is especially distasteful should he be forced to employ a strange, foreign unit, with which he is totally unacquainted, and to which orders must be transmitted in a foreign tongue through an interpreter. However, whatever the problems presented, I had no option but to carry out the instructions I had received from the Theatre Commander. The attack launched … was surprisingly enough successful. It penetrated for some distance, all the way to Sitapur on the edge of Myitkyina itself … Immediately counterattacked from all sides, by the highly mobile Japanese floating reserve, this small unit dug in and established a small perimeter. Attempts to supply it with ammunition and food failed because of the small area available as a target. (Hunter 1963, pp. 157–58)

American troops lead their pack animals laden with supplies and weapons to forward areas from Myitkyina airfield. A C-47 Dakota transport is in the background. (NARA RG 208-AA-12B-3)

Hunter also mobilized his remaining Marauders from H Force and these elements, rather than waiting for aerial resupply, set out for their assigned destinations on the outskirts of the town of Myitkyina. Early on May 18, White Combat Team of H Force occupied Rampur. Osborne then moved on to Zigyun and occupied it without opposition, waiting for two days for the Chinese infantry to relieve them so that the Marauders could return to the airfield. Kinnison's K Force, closing in on Myitkyina from the north, arrived at the Myitkyina–Mogaung motor road at first light on May 19. Under Merrill's orders, Kinnison attacked and captured the village of Charpate without much opposition; he then ordered his 3d Marauder Battalion to block the road from Mogaung as well as the trails leading into the now-occupied village, but thickly vegetated high ground 400–500yd to the northwest was not taken. The Marauder forces were so positioned in an arc covering trails and roads to the northwest that Japanese reinforcements could only reach Myitkyina from across the Irrawaddy River to the east or from Nsopzup to the northeast via the Myitkyina–Mankrin or Myitkyina–Radhapur roads. After establishing this perimeter, Merrill formed Myitkyina Task Force by dissolving H and K forces and merging all Marauder battalions together under Hunter. The Chinese regiments were under separate control. The Japanese, meanwhile, had been able to reinforce the Myitkyina garrison. An estimated 3,000 to 4,000 enemy troops had come in from the Nsopzup, Mogaung, and Bhamo areas. The Japanese had built up more strength at Myitkyina than the Allies, enabling them to start offensive maneuvering.

On May 21, the Marauder 3d Battalion was ordered to take Myitkyina's auxiliary airstrip to the northeast. It came up against strong enemy positions, necessitating the Marauders to dig in. After a Japanese attack against his rear was thwarted by Allied artillery support, Beach withdrew the 3d Battalion to its original position at Charpate. For the next two days, the 3d Battalion fought off repeated enemy attacks, but on orders from Hunter, they withdrew on May 24 to the railroad two miles to the south. The Japanese quickly occupied Charpate and prepared to hold it in force.

On May 26, the Japanese, under the cover of a mortar barrage, attacked Namkwi in force and compelled the Marauder 2d Battalion to retreat to a ridgeline halfway to Myitkyina. As at Charpate, the Japanese quickly occupied Namkwi and set up extensive defensive fortifications. The reinvigorated enemy had taken over two towns on the way to Myitkyina. On May 27, McGee's 2d Battalion was sent out again to reach Radhapur, with an attached Company C of the 209th Engineer Combat Battalion; however, with most of the Marauders suffering from fatigue, dysentery, malaria, and malnutrition, the unit was no longer able to participate in

American soldiers peer out of a captured pillbox along the siege lines established to capture Myitkyina town. A discarded Japanese helmet and chipped bayonet lie discarded on the ground in front of them. (USAMHI).

A Chinese artillery crew fires their 105mm howitzer at Japanese positions during the siege of Myitkyina. The Allied attack force was not sufficiently strong to capture the town, and so a siege had to be implemented as ground forces and artillery were gradually airlanded at the captured strip. Instead of combat troops, Lieutenant-General Stratemeyer, FEAF, had initially sent in an aviation engineer battalion to improve the strip and a battalion of British antiaircraft artillery to defend it. (NARA 111-SC-192537)

combat. In fact, most of the Galahad force was unfit for further combat operations by June. Of the 1,310 Marauders who reached Myitkyina airfield on May 17, over half had been evacuated to rear echelon hospitals by June 1. Only about 200 men of the 1st Battalion remained until the fall of Myitkyina town on August 3.

Having yet again fallen ill, Merrill's leadership role was assumed by his headquarters deputy Colonel John E. McCammon. On May 22, McCammon was promoted by Stilwell to brigadier-general, giving him command status over all the Myitkyina area units, American and Chinese. "Stilwell decided against the logical choice of appointing Hunter [Merrill's] successor and instead went for another 'yes man', the amiable but inexperienced Col John McCammon, who immediately got off on the wrong foot with Hunter by inquiring: 'What are your plans for withdrawal if the stuff hits the fan?'" (Mortimer 2013, p. 182). Hunter would act as McCammon's executive officer and commander of the Galahad contingent of the Allied Myitkyina Task Force (MTF).

Another Stilwell decision also affected the campaign for Myitkyina town early on. Although a quick seizure of Myitkyina would enable him to attack the rear of the Japanese forces on the Salween front, Stilwell briefly considered asking that the veteran British 36th Division be rushed in to take Myitkyina. The 36th Division was ready to fly in, as it later did, to take the "Railway Corridor," and could have been put into Myitkyina airfield at short notice; the British infantrymen were fit and ready for battle and were the obvious force with which to replace Hunter's exhausted men. Stilwell negated using this fine British formation and left no rationale for it in his diary. Instead he ordered in US combat engineers from the Ledo Road construction project, telling

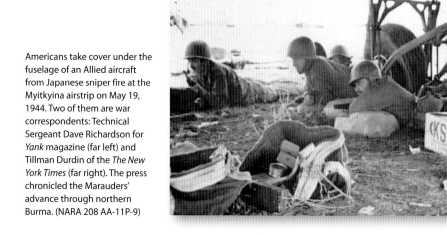

Americans take cover under the fuselage of an Allied aircraft from Japanese sniper fire at the Myitkyina airstrip on May 19, 1944. Two of them are war correspondents: Technical Sergeant Dave Richardson for *Yank* magazine (far left) and Tillman Durdin of the *The New York Times* (far right). The press chronicled the Marauders' advance through northern Burma. (NARA 208 AA-11P-9)

Marshall, "I will probably have to use some of our engineer units to keep an American flavor in the fight" (Romanus and Sunderland 1970, p. 228). With a dozen war correspondents on the Myitkyina airfield disseminating news to the world of his great American victory, "it was unthinkable for Stilwell to call on the British to pick his chestnuts out of the fire" (Allen 2000, p. 367).

The Japanese reinforcement of Myitkyina was rapid. Maruyama's force in the town expanded to approximately 4,500. Maruyama, using the Irrawaddy as a "ferry service," much like the Soviets used the Volga at Stalingrad, brought in major elements of the 56th Division from the Salween front into Myitkyina on the May 17 order of General Honda (Thirty-third Army commander). Control of Japanese operations at Myitkyina was assumed by Honda's army in early June, allowing Tanaka to concentrate his attention on operations around Kamaing. A group of Chindits, Morris Force, was supposed to interdict Japanese movement to the western bank of the river; however, they proved incapable of this challenging task. With this troop transfer, Mizukami assumed overall command in Myitkyina with the specific order to hold the town at all costs. Mizukami also reinforced the Myitkyina garrison with other elements of the 3/114th Infantry Regiment, then in the Pinbaw area, to the southwest of Mogaung. Mizukami reached Myitkyina on May 30 with the infantry reinforcement arriving between June 4 and 8. "Some of Stilwell's key American subordinates in the MTF asserted that faulty, repetitive underestimates of the Japanese garrison's strength led to poor tactical and strategic decision making that necessitated the lengthy siege" (quoted in Diamond 2013, p. 24) and were about to snatch victory from Stilwell's hands. The discrepancy between the intelligence estimates harbored by the senior MTF commanders at Naubum and the true figures angered Hunter to such a degree that he stated after the war that the low estimates were "to deceive the Chinese troops into a sense of shame in view of their demonstrated lack of aggressiveness. Neither the Chinese nor Galahad fell for this intelligence" (quoted in Diamond 2013, p. 67).

A Japanese soldier acting as a human antitank/antipersonnel mine in an entrenched hole. He has a 100lb bomb between his knees and holds a piece of steel to act as a detonator. He was killed by infantry rifle fire before he could detonate the device. (NARA RG 208AA 248 BB)

A C-47 Dakota transport takes off from the Myitkyina airstrip during the latter part of the 73-day siege of Myitkyina town. The P-40N fighters lining the runway belong to the 88th Fighter Squadron. (USAMHI)

Also, the Japanese were reinforcing Myitkyina more quickly than the Allies could, in large part due to the rain, which often closed the Myitkyina field to C-47 troop carrier planes. With only a dozen P-40s now at Myitkyina, along with a paucity of artillery pieces and no tanks, it would be nearly impossible to break into the Japanese entrenchments, especially with the continuation of steady rainfall. The Japanese were not merely static, but made repeated attacks on the Allied positions in late May. After a failed

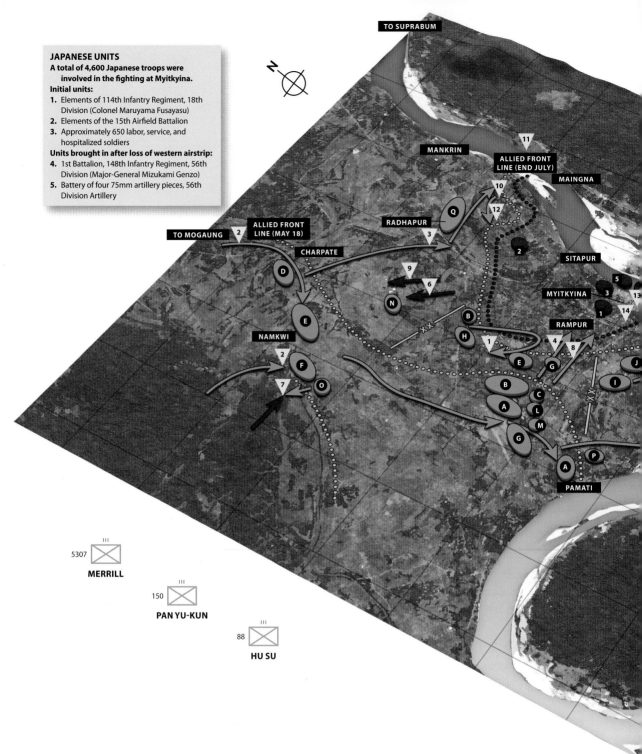

TO SUPRABUM

MANKRIN

ALLIED FRONT
LINE (END JULY)

MAINGNA

RADHAPUR

ALLIED FRONT
LINE (MAY 18)

TO MOGAUNG

CHARPATE

SITAPUR

MYITKYINA

RAMPUR

NAMKWI

PAMATI

5307   MERRILL

150   PAN YU-KUN

88   HU SU

ASSAULT ON MYITKYINA, MAY 18–AUGUST 3, 1944

The terrain around Myitkyina was excellent for defense and the Japanese took every advantage of it. The roads lay high above the surrounding rice paddies, and each became an embankment that could be turned into a fortified position. Although Stilwell would eventually conduct what amounted to a siege of Myitkyina town, the Japanese received small amounts of supplies and reinforcements via a ferry service across the Irrawaddy, and from the west until Mogaung fell on June 26. The situation was one where Stilwell's besieging force was surrounded by enemy-held territory.

18 [XX] (-)

TANAKA

114 [III] (-)

MARUYAMA

WAINGMAW

5

B

A

ZIGYUN

ALLIED UNITS

Initial units in overland assault:

H Force (Colonel Hunter):
A. 1st Battalion, 5307th Composite Unit (Provisional)
B. Chinese 150th Infantry Regiment, 50th Division (plus 3d Company, Animal Transport Regiment)
C. Battery of the Chinese 22d Division Artillery

K Force (Colonel Kinnison):
D. 3d Battalion, 5307th Composite Unit (Provisional)
E. Chinese 88th Infantry Regiment, 30th Division

M Force (Colonel McGee):
F. 2d Battalion, 5307th Composite Unit (Provisional) (plus 300 Kachin scouts)

Units airlanded at Myitkyina airfield:

G. Chinese 2d Battalion, 89th Infantry Regiment, 30th Division
H. Elements of Chinese 90th Infantry Regiment, 30th Division
I. Chinese 3d Battalion, 42d Infantry Regiment, 14th Division
J. Chinese 2d Battalion, 41st Infantry Regiment, 14th Division
K. Elements of the Chinese 149th Infantry Regiment, 50th Division
L. W and X troops of the British 69th Light (Anti-Aircraft) Regiment
M. 879th Engineer Aviation Battalion
N. 209th Engineer Combat Battalion
O. 236th Engineer Combat Battalion
P. 504th Engineer Light Pontoon Company
Q. Reinforcements for the 5307th from India (*c.*2,600 men – "New Galahad")

Other Allied resources present:
14 75mm, 2 105mm and 2 155mm artillery pieces; 12 P-40s of the 88th Fighter Squadron; Seagrave and 42d Portable Surgical Hospital units.

▼ EVENTS

1. May 18, 1200hrs: the Chinese 150th Infantry Regiment, 50th Division, is sent towards Myitkyina, but after some confused "friendly-fire" encounters, this force retreats from the town.

2. May 19: the Chinese 88th Infantry Regiment, 30th Division, seizes Charpate, northwest of Myitkyina, and extends its lines south to the railroad tracks. Also on this day, M Force takes the settlement of Namkwi to the southwest of Charpate.

3. May 21: the 3d Battalion of the 5307th is ordered to take the auxiliary airstrip due north of Myitkyina; however, its troops fail to reach their objective and dig in along the Mankrin–Radhapur road. That night, the Marauders are attacked by the Japanese from the west and are forced to retire to Charpate. The Chinese 88th and 89th Infantry regiments are deployed on either side of the tracks of the Myitkyina–Mogaung railroad.

4. May 25, 0700hrs: the Chinese 88th and 89th Infantry regiments are ordered to attack Myitkyina through to the riverbank, which the Japanese have been using to ferry in reinforcements across the Irrawaddy. The attack only accomplishes a straightening of 88th Infantry Regiment's lines.

5. May 31: elements of the Chinese 42d Infantry Regiment, 14th Division, reach the Waingmaw ferry road. The Japanese are firmly entrenched on a 12ft embankment overlooking rice paddy fields. The Chinese retreat, but manage to thwart an enemy counterattack. The Chinese 150th Infantry Regiment reaches the riverbank and the Chinese units draw up in an arc around the Japanese strongpoint at a sawmill.

6. May 31, night: Japanese troops attack the 209th Engineer Combat Battalion at Radhapur, north of Myitkyina.

7. June 1: the American 236th Engineer Combat Battalion is sent to retake Namkwi from the Japanese attacking from the west; however, only one company enters the village before being quickly evicted by a Japanese counterattack.

8. June 3: elements of the 42d, 150th and 89th Chinese Infantry regiments attack Myitkyina, but after incurring over 300 casualties the attack is called off. Siege warfare, at times with tunneling, is implemented with an arc of Chinese and American forces surrounding Myitkyina by the night of June 13.

9. June 13–14: A and B companies of the 209th Engineer Combat Battalion are surrounded by Japanese counterattacks between Myitkyina and Radhapur.

10. June 17: the 3d Battalion of the 5307th cuts the Maingna ferry road north of Myitkyina along the Irrawaddy. Apart from a major unsuccessful attack on July 12, fighting is sporadic and daily gains are measured in yards. The Allied lines are steadily constricting around Myitkyina.

11. July 22: eight rafts and a boat laden with Japanese wounded attempting to flee Myitkyina are attacked on the Irrawaddy by Kachins of OSS Detachment 101. The Japanese are beginning to succumb to the siege.

12. July 26–27: the 3d Battalion of the 5307th, largely comprising reinforcements and termed "New Galahad," crosses the crescent-shaped swamp area north of Myitkyina and takes the northern airstrip.

13. July 29–31: Allied attacks, encountering weaker Japanese resistance, make deeper advances into the enemy lines. On August 1, General Mizukami commits suicide after making his apologies to the Japanese emperor.

14. August 3, 1545: resistance by the Japanese rear guard slackens, and the surrounding Allied regiments advance speedily to capture the town. Colonel Maruyama, commanding officer of the III/114th Infantry Regiment of the 18th Division, escapes with approximately 600 Japanese troops.

A desolate area on the outskirts of Myitkyina town, part of a Japanese entrenchment network. This area was held for four weeks, despite Allied attacks. (USAMHI)

A Chinese soldier surveys Japanese destroyed entrenchments. The wooden beams and corrugated tin roofs provided a degree of protection from mortar rounds but not Allied fighter-bomber sorties or heavier artillery such as the 75 and 105mm howitzers. (NARA 559282 MM 229)

assault through Myitkyina by the Chinese 88th and 89th Infantry regiments on May 25, Stilwell replaced McCammon with Boatner on May 30. Throughout this "see-saw" conflict of May, Galahad had exhausted itself and suffered a complete decline in morale.

Stilwell was beginning to face the disheartening fact that a protracted struggle was to develop to capture Myitkyina town. He started to search his CBI theater for additional troops. The Tenth Air Force at once gave over the remainder of its 879th Airborne Engineer Aviation Battalion to repair and hold the vital airfield, the only means of contact between the MTF and the rear echelons back in the Hukawng Valley or Assam. Then, Stilwell turned to Pick for additional engineers to be employed as combat infantry at Myitkyina. On May 19, Lieutenant William D. Flatley and a detachment from the 504th Engineer Light Pontoon Company flew in from Ledo to set up operations on the Irrawaddy, south of the airfield at Pamati. When the depleted Marauder ranks frantically called for reinforcements in their perimeter northwest of Myitkyina as the resurgent Japanese were counterattacking, Stilwell responded by ordering the 209th Engineer Battalion onto C-47 transports bound for Myitkyina airfield. Two days later, the 236th Combat Engineer Battalion, Pick's sole remaining combat engineer formation, was reassigned for infantry service in the mounting struggle at Myitkyina. More Chinese infantrymen were thrown into the attack too, but the enemy – stronger than American intelligence had surmised – was digging in tenaciously on a robust perimeter and executing intermittent local counterattacks.

"June deteriorated into a month of frustration as the monsoon interfered with resupply operations" (Hunter 1963, p. 161). On June 3, the Chinese 42d and 150th Infantry regiments attacked the town, only to be pushed back by the Japanese after heavy casualties. American intelligence officers began sensing that the Japanese garrison was stronger than expected, but clung to the estimate that only 1,000 Japanese combat troops faced them. On June 17, Galahad's 3d Battalion reached the Irrawaddy River north of Myitkyina, having moved against the auxiliary airstrip on May 21. This gain coincided with further advances by the Chinese 150th Infantry Regiment. At the same time, the Americans captured the Myitkyina–Mogaung–Sumprabum road junction. However, because of increasing manpower losses among the Americans and Chinese, Stilwell ordered a halt to his infantry attacks and resorted to tunneling. The Chinese troops had even attempted mining operations. For Stilwell's troops, daily progress was measured in yards. As the Marauder ranks were slowly being depleted, the rear area combat engineers, hastily ordered to Myitkyina, were no replacement for the veterans of Galahad, although after being "blooded," the 209th and 236th Combat Engineers fought with greater élan. These two units would sustain casualty rates as heavy as any other combat unit during the global conflict.

A Chinese soldier takes aim with his rifle at a sniper hiding in a series of destroyed railroad boxcars in Myitkyina town. (USAMHI)

Throughout the remainder of June, a battle of attrition raged as combat and disease exhausted both sides. With little progress being made and with Boatner requiring evacuation for malaria, Brigadier-General Theodore F. Wessels took over the command of MTF on June 26. At SEAC headquarters, Wessels had been tasked with training the next 30 Chinese divisions. Coincident with Wessels' appointment, Calvert's 77th Indian Infantry Brigade captured Mogaung, which enabled the Chinese troops that had arrived there to now move up the railroad and join the MTF's beleaguered forces. "This was a great gift of fortune. It removed the recurrent menace of a Japanese drive from Mogaung, guaranteed reinforcements and the opening of a ground line of communications, and meant that Wessels' men, instead of being an island in a hostile sea open to attack from 3,600, could concentrate their attention on the Japanese to their front" (Romanus and Sunderland 1970, p. 249).

Wessels launched a major attack on July 12 with air support; however, it failed, necessitating a return to the slow slugfest, which drove the Japanese back on a daily basis. The initial signs that the Japanese force at Myitkyina was beginning to lose the battle for the town occurred during the last week of July when Japanese wounded were being floated down the Irrawaddy via raft and key IJA officers were committing ritual suicide. When elements of the Marauder's 3d Battalion captured the northern airfield at Myitkyina on July 26, Japanese resistance was noticeably weaker. On August 1, Stilwell

A Chinese soldier with his Enfield P-17 rifle slung over his shoulder searches for Japanese soldiers hiding in the destroyed railroad boxcar in Myitkyina town. (NARA 559282 MM 225)

was promoted to four-star general. Also on that day, after he had made sure that the main part of his defenders, under Maruyama, could be safely withdrawn from the area, Mizukami Genzo committed suicide. On August 3, Wessels ordered a fresh attack on the town and Myitkyina was finally captured. The Japanese had left a small rearguard of fewer than 200 sick men, some of whom ended their own lives rather than surrender to the enemy. Maruyama was able to withdraw 600 men. The Americans suffered a total of 2,207 casualties while those of their Chinese comrades amounted to 4,344. The Japanese suffered 790 killed, 1,180 wounded, and 187 captured.

An American soldier takes a drink in front of a fallen building sign in Myitkyina town. Myitkyina was both a transportation and commerce hub being situated on the great Irrawaddy River, as well as the terminus of the Mandalay–Myitkyina Burmese railway. (USAMHI)

An aerial view of the devastation wreaked upon Myitkyina town with destroyed railway cars and tracks in the foreground and the Irrawaddy River in the background. A checkerboard pattern of dirt tracks is apparent, but the houses that were once present have been destroyed. (NARA 559282 MM 224)

Myitkyina airfield was seized with a precise, surprise attack; however, what could have been a rapid follow-up capture of the town never materialized due to faulty planning, a lack of interservice cooperation, and, perhaps, the manipulation of intelligence, resulting in a grueling ten-week siege. Hunter concluded: "I still believe that the mission of my task force [H] should have been to capture the city rather than the airstrip. Had the city been taken the word would have gotten around and the area would not have become a rallying point for all the remaining Japanese in northeast Burma. The field would have been untenable [for the local Japanese defenders] with the city in our hands" (Hunter 1963, p. 180). Hunter believed that the airstrip at Myitkyina was not a natural terrain feature that facilitated either temporary defense or continuing offensive action. Myitkyina town, on the banks of the Irrawaddy, did. In fact, "there were days in which a banzai charge by General Mizukami's garrison or a determined push by the 53rd Division, which had been ordered to send a regiment and lift the siege, would in all probability have swept right over the airstrip" (Romanus and Sunderland 1970, p. 244).

As for the MTF, Boatner reflected: "the number of our troops gave a deceiving picture of our real strength. The four regiments of Chinese came from the 30th, 14th, and 50th divisions. They could not compare with the regiments in the veteran 38th and 22nd divisions in experience, training and firepower. The 14th and 50th divisions arrived in Burma direct from China only in April ... The U.S. troops consisted of two separate battalions of Engineers and newly arrived replacements for Galahad, the veterans of which had mostly been evacuated. So our forces were a hodge-podge collection of fine men but inexperienced in combat and completely unprepared for attacking the veteran Japanese" (Boatner 1971, pp. 46–47). Stilwell wrote to Marshall: "Our own artillery was very, very weak ... Only four 75 millimeter howitzers the first few weeks, then some 4.2 inch mortars and only in the last few weeks about two 155s came in. Our air combat support could not be relied upon for an integrated attack because of their commitments elsewhere and almost daily hindrance by intervening mountains" (Boatner 1971, p. 47). Air transport delivery of artillery was compromised by the monsoon and poor airstrip conditions, which wrecked a number of C-47 planes, and severely hampered resupply. Succinctly put, the MTF had "less than a battalion of artillery for a major operation" (Hunter 1963, p. 201).

AFTERMATH

Stilwell's overland advance and the Chindits' Operation Thursday during 1944 defeated the IJA in northern Burma and enabled the capture of Myitkyina airfield in a *coup de main*. For a variety of reasons, including Stilwell's refusal to use the excellent British 36th Division in his assault, an additional 78 days were needed for the Chinese–American forces to take Myitkyina town while the debilitated Chindit brigades and surviving Marauders were evacuated to India after months of combat, malnutrition, and disease, which decimated their ranks and future capabilities as fighting units. Parenthetically, the 36th Division was the first all-British unit to come under the command of General Joseph Stilwell and its task, in the summer of 1944, was to clear the "Railway Corridor" – a stretch of terrain through which the Burma Railway ran from the area of the Mu River Valley in the south and extending north past Wuntho, Mawlu, Indaw, and Katha for roughly 160 miles, where it opened up into the valley of the Mogaung River and on to Myitkyina.

A truck convoy is halted along the Ledo Road by a mudslide. Drainage of the road was always a persistent problem, as evidenced by a piece of a culvert tube lying to the left of the road surface. (USAMHI)

The taking of Myitkyina on August 3, 1944 made possible an intensified air effort from bases in China in support of American operations in the Pacific. It also reclaimed a portion of the Burmese road network, which linked with the Burma Road. One part of the American mission to China also called for the Ledo Road and pipeline from India to join the Burma Road and re-establish the overland route to deliver adequate supplies and fuel to Chiang Kai-shek's Nationalist forces combating the Japanese there. Stilwell's task to capture Myitkyina and bring the Ledo Road and pipeline close to the Burma Road was accomplished, despite many of his contemporaries thinking it was an impossible one. Ultimately, further Allied advances down the "Railway Corridor" and a Chinese offensive from Yunnan would eventually drive out the last Japanese, and the existing road from Myitkyina, now connected to Assam via the Ledo Road, could be re-established to effectively end the Japanese land blockade of China.

Stilwell was a troop trainer and a tactician, not an engineer. The construction of the Ledo Road, although under Stilwell's overall command, was conducted by the engineering and supply marvels Lewis Pick and Major-General Raymond Wheeler (Commanding General, Services of Supply, CBI) respectively. By October 2, one of the two pipelines was in operation from the Indian refineries via Ledo to Myitkyina. Henceforth, Myitkyina would become a key supply center fed by road, air, and by pipeline.

As a result of the northern Burma campaign's efforts, the Allies would certainly be able to comply with Roosevelt and Marshall's directives to "Support China" and keep it in the war. On January 12, 1945, the first truck convoy from Ledo to China – "Pick's First Convoy" – started its 1,100-mile trek. The two-week trip crossed the Patkai Hills in easternmost India, before traversing the Hukawng Valley, replete with swamps and rivers. The Ledo Road would pass Stilwell's first field headquarters in northern Burma at Shingbwiyang, just over 100 miles from its Indian origin. "Pick's Pike" would also cross the junction of the Tarung and Tanai hkas, via newly constructed pontoon and road bridges, which was the site of Tanaka's river outposts that stalemated Stilwell from October 1943 to January 1944 near Yupbang Ga. Extending southwards through the Hukawng Valley, the truck convoy passed near Walawbum, where the first envelopment was launched by the Marauders on Tanaka's 18th Division infantry. The Ledo Road, having traversed the Jambu Bum ridgeline, entered the Mogaung Valley past Inkangahtawng and Kamaing, where Tanaka fought Stilwell's Sino-American force with essentially three regiments. As the Ledo Road passed Mogaung, the Burmese town that was captured by (but almost destroyed) the Chindit's 77th Indian Infantry Brigade, it descended into the Irrawaddy Valley only miles away from Myitkyina. There, the Ledo Road was still only 25 percent of the way to Kunming in China. Due to continued Japanese resistance south of Myitkyina, the Ledo Road would not reach the Burma Road at Mong Yu and enter the Chinese town of Wanting in Yunnan Province until January 28, 1945. At the Yunnan terminus, the combined Ledo and Burma roads were renamed the "Stilwell Road" by none other than Chiang Kai-shek.

Some cynics would contend that the "Stilwell Road" overland supply route from India to China had become obsolete as, by the end of January 1945, the Allied CCS had instead decided to attack Japan from the home islands, and not from the Chinese mainland or Formosa. Although the northern Burma campaign of

The first truck convoy to traverse "Pick's Pike" enters Wanting, China in January 1945 on the reopened Burma Road. (USAMHI)

1943–44 has been mislabeled as a military backwater by some in contrast to other massive battlefields during the global conflict, it needs to be emphasized that Allied division and corps-sized forces engaged in deadly, protracted combat over several months at the extreme end of the logistical supply chain in some of the harshest terrain and climate imaginable. As a result of the Allied victory in northern Burma, not only was the Japanese retreat from Imphal eastwards miserable due to a lack of supplies and transport, but it greatly contributed to the ability for Slim to launch his offensive into Central Burma after securing victories at Imphal and Kohima. By early 1945, on the Arakan Peninsula in southwest Burma, the British and Indians were now retaking land from the Japanese with great leaps towards Rangoon. In central Burma, Slim's forces had crossed the Shwebo Plain and were now arrayed near the Irrawaddy at several spots ready to entrap General Kimura Heitaro's forces and secure victory at Meiktila and recapture Mandalay.

As for Stilwell, with the capture of Myitkyina he was promoted to a four-star general, a rank held at that time only by Marshall, MacArthur, Arnold, and Eisenhower. However, with the success of a Japanese land offensive, Operation *Ichigo*, in east China, coupled with a rancorous dispute with General Claire Chennault, and Marshall's plan for sending Stilwell to China to take over command of the retreating Chinese armies there, a smoldering political firestorm was underway.

A Japanese soldier who preferred to honor the bushido or warrior code by committing suicide rather than surrendering to his enemies. (USAMHI)

Chiang Kai-shek had made Stilwell's new assignment predicated on Chinese, not Stilwell's, control of all Lend-Lease supplies. Several days after Stilwell hand-delivered a sharp communique from Roosevelt to Chiang on September 19, 1944 with much hubris, the Generalissimo decided that Stilwell had to be dismissed. After much political maneuvering, on October 18 Roosevelt agreed to Chiang's request for Stilwell's immediate recall, which was relayed to Stilwell the next day. The CBI theater was to be divided among a handful of American generals serving the roles that Stilwell had done individually.

A report by an IJA 56th Infantry Regiment commander on June 7, 1944 gave an account of the demise of Tanaka's famed 18th Division on the Kamaing Road near the Chinese infantry roadblock at Seton:

> The advance attack of the enemy from the north is unexpectedly swift; the enemy is advancing southwards, threading through the gaps in our lines by wading chest-high through

marshy zones. I am unable to get in touch with 1st and 3d Battalions, which are under my command, and their situation is unknown. The platoon occupying the vicinity of Nanyaseik received an enemy onslaught and all troops were annihilated. The enemy stormed into our main artillery position, and with our motor trucks, artillery and other vehicles crowded together in the vicinity of the narrow, forked road, there is much confusion. The transfer of most of the patients has been completed. The regiment will cover the withdrawal of the main body of the division at the sacrifice of our lives. I believe this will be our final parting. Please give best regards to the division commander. (Romanus and Sunderland 1970, p. 218)

Of the 18th Division and the two additional units under Tanaka's command – the 4th and 146th Infantry regiments – only 5,000 men succeeded in escaping to the southeast, then back to the sheltering hills. The 18th Division lost 50 percent of the strength with which it began its attempt to repel the Allied advance in north Burma.

FURTHER READING

Allen, Louis, Burma: *The Longest War 1941–45*, Phoenix Press: London, 2000
Bidwell, Shelford, *The Chindit War: Stilwell, Wingate, and the Campaign in Burma: 1944*, MacMillan Publishing Co.: New York, 1979
Boatner, Haydon L., *Haydon L. Boatner Papers, 1900–1971*, United States Army Military History Institute: Carlisle Barracks, 1971
Callahan, Raymond, *Burma 1942–1945*, University of Delaware Press: Newark, 1978
Calvert, Michael, *Prisoners of Hope*, Pen & Sword: London, 1996
Chinnery, Philip D., *March or Die*, Airlife Publishing Ltd: Shrewsbury, 1997
Churchill, Winston S., *Closing the Ring: The Second World War, Volume 5*, Houghton, Mifflin Company: Boston, 1951
Diamond, Jon, *Orde Wingate*, Osprey Publishing Ltd.: Oxford, 2012
——, "Blunder or Deception," *WWII History*, Sovereign Media: McClean, December 2013
Eldridge, Fred, *Wrath in Burma: The Uncensored Story of General Stilwell and International Maneuvers in the Far East*, Doubleday & Company, Inc.: Garden City, 1946
Hunter, Charles N., *Galahad*, The Naylor Company: San Antonio, 1963
——, *Galahad: Intelligence Aspects*, CIA Historical Review Program: Langley, 1993
Jeffrey, W. F., *Sunbeams Like Swords*, Hodder and Stoughton: London, 1950
Madej, W. Victor (ed.), *Japanese Armed Forces Order of Battle 1937–1945*, Allentown: Game Marketing Co., 1981
McGee, George A., *The History of the Second Battalion*, privately published, 1987
McKelvie, Roy, *The War in Burma*, Methuen & Co.: London, 1948
McLynn, Frank, *The Burma Campaign: Disaster into Triumph 1942–45*, Yale University Press: New Haven and London, 2011
Mortimer, Gavin, *Merrill's Marauders*, Zenith Press: Minneapolis, 2013
Ogburn, Charlton, *The Marauders*, Quill: New York, 1982
Romanus, Charles F. and Sunderland, Riley, *Stilwell's Command Problems*, US Government Printing Office: Washington, DC, 1970
Rooney, David, *Stilwell the Patriot: Vinegar Joe, the Brits, and Chiang Kai-shek*, Greenhill Books: London, 2005
Sacquety, Troy J., *The OSS in Burma: Jungle War Against the Japanese*, University Press of Kansas: Kansas, 2013
Stilwell, Joseph W. (ed. Theodore H. White), *The Stilwell Papers*, Da Capo Press: New York, 1991
Thompson, Julian, *The Imperial War Museum Book of the War in Burma 1942–1945*, Pan Books: London, 2003
Tuchman, Barbara W., *Stilwell and the American Experience in China 1911–1945*, MacMillan: New York, 1970

INDEX